CULTURE SMART!

INDIA

THE ESSENTIAL GUIDE TO CUSTOMS & CULTURE

BECKY STEPHEN

KUPERARD

"The real voyage of discovery consists not in seeking new landscapes, but in having new eyes."

Adapted from Marcel Proust, *Remembrance of Things Past.*

ISBN 978 1 78702 900 2

British Library Cataloguing in Publication Data
A CIP catalogue entry for this book is available
from the British Library

First published in Great Britain
by Kuperard, an imprint of Bravo Ltd
59 Hutton Grove, London N12 8DS
Tel: +44 (0) 20 8446 2440
www.culturesmart.co.uk
Inquiries: publicity@kuperard.co.uk

Design Bobby Birchall
Printed in Turkey

ABOUT THE AUTHOR

BECKY STEPHEN was born in the US as an "air force brat," growing up in several states, as well as in England. Long fascinated by Indian culture and philosophy, Becky moved to India in 1988 to study Hindi at Banaras Hindu University, Varanasi. She met her South Indian husband there and ended up living in Varanasi for five years.

Becky has a Masters in Intercultural Studies from Fuller Theological Seminary, Pasadena, California, and has developed and led cross-cultural and other training programs and events in the US, India, Eurasia, Europe, and the Arabian Peninsula. After working for three years in Dubai as a management consultant and cross-cultural trainer, she moved with her husband and son to Atlanta, Georgia, where she trains and supervises Americans on long-term international assignments.

CONTENTS

MAP OF INDIA

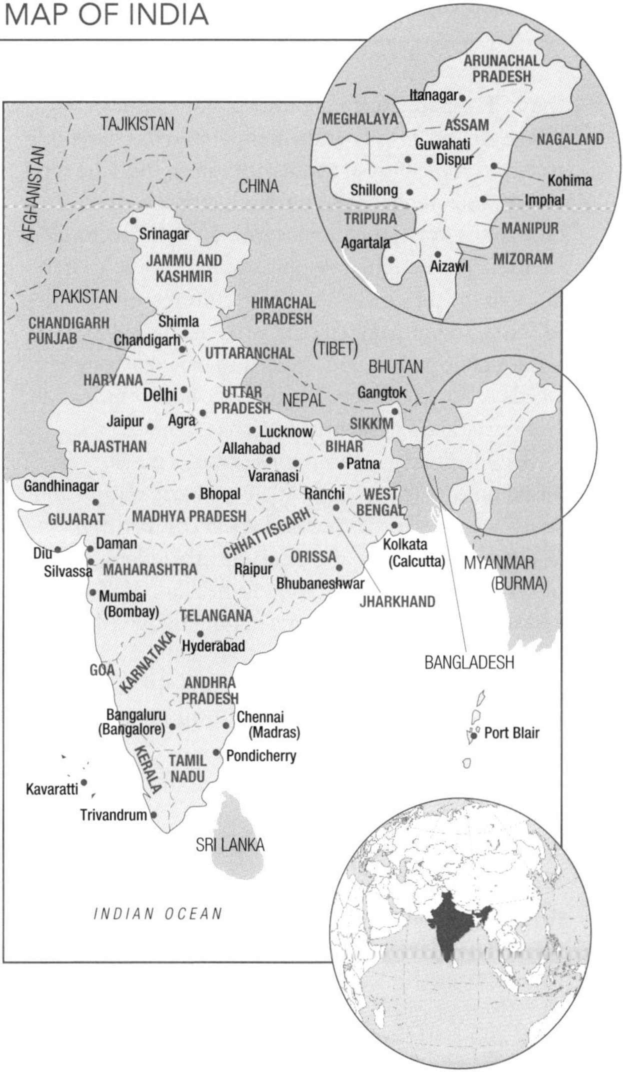
ARUNACHAL PRADESH
Itanagar
MEGHALAYA
ASSAM
NAGALAND
Guwahati
Dispur
Kohima
Shillong
Imphal
TRIPURA
MANIPUR
Agartala
Aizawl
MIZORAM
TAJIKISTAN
AFGHANISTAN
CHINA
Srinagar
JAMMU AND KASHMIR
PAKISTAN
HIMACHAL PRADESH
CHANDIGARH
Shimla
PUNJAB
Chandigarh
UTTARANCHAL
(TIBET)
BHUTAN
HARYANA
Delhi
UTTAR PRADESH
NEPAL
Gangtok
Jaipur
Agra
SIKKIM
Lucknow
RAJASTHAN
Allahabad
BIHAR
Patna
Varanasi
Gandhinagar
Bhopal
Ranchi
WEST BENGAL
GUJARAT
MADHYA PRADESH
CHHATTISGARH
Daman
Kolkata (Calcutta)
Diu
ORISSA
Silvassa
MAHARASHTRA
Raipur
MYANMAR (BURMA)
Bhubaneshwar
Mumbai (Bombay)
JHARKHAND
TELANGANA
Hyderabad
BANGLADESH
GOA
KARNATAKA
ANDHRA PRADESH
Bangaluru (Bangalore)
Chennai (Madras)
Port Blair
KERALA
TAMIL NADU
Pondicherry
Kavaratti
Trivandrum
SRI LANKA
INDIAN OCEAN

India. The name instantly evokes associations and images in our minds. India has painted its colors on nearly every aspect of modern Western life. The food we eat, how we decorate our homes, what we wear, how we exercise, the movies we watch, the technology we use, and the religious options available to us have all been influenced by the many cultures and peoples of India. Indian languages have even entered our vocabulary: pundit, jodhpurs, and pajamas were Hindi words taken up by the British Raj; catamaran, pariah, and curry are Tamil contributions.

Seen from afar, perceptions of India may be based on overwhelming statistics on population and snapshots of poverty; technological competition in the global market; exotic art forms; and ancient history. All this is true. But at its heart, India is its people. Mother India's nearly 1.4 billion "children" are as varied and colorful as the spice markets of Old Delhi. Each region, caste, and community has its own culture, reflecting unique histories shaped by conquest, creativity, and religion, expressed in distinct languages, social customs, art forms, and expectations of life.

In the face of five-thousand-year-old traditions, India is changing. Yet, despite enormous changes, in many ways it remains the same—a total sensory experience. The chaos and beauty of color and sound, the language shifts every ten miles, the household variations of spice and spiciness, the insistent smells of everyday life lived very much in public, and the invasion of personal space will challenge the most experienced traveler. But it is in surrender to your senses that you begin to embrace the essence of India.

As you experience India up close, you will begin to understand something of the seemingly infinite capacity of Indians to live with paradox. The spectacle of India's proud traditions and the Indians' love for their land is commingled with tensions and prejudices rooted in conquests and rivalries long past. Ancient temples decorated with intricate sculptures may be plastered with signs advertising the latest technologies. You will smell the burgeoning slums that have been part of the rapid urbanization of the last century, and meet an affluent middle class that was nonexistent before the last few decades. You'll taste the metallic tang of pollution as your auto rickshaw darts through traffic, competing with delicious aromas steaming from the vats of street vendors.

Steeped in tradition, exceptionally fatalistic, and intensely passionate about their culture, Indians are some of the most ingenious, adventurous, and creative people on the planet. Warm and friendly, most will respond to your interest in them and their country with generosity and genuine friendship. But they also have indelible ties to family and community that form boundary lines and determine decisions that do not always seem reasonable from the outside.

Visitors' responses to India can be as extreme as the people and places they encounter there. This book aims to make you aware of the basic values and behavioral norms, to show you how to navigate cultural differences and connect with real people, and to offer insights into the endlessly fascinating place that is India.

Country Name	Republic of India	In Hindi, Bharatiya Ganarajya (Bharat)
Capital	New Delhi	Old Delhi (Shahjahanabad), in the heart of New Delhi, was the Mughal capital.
Most Populated Cities	Mumbai 18.4 million Kolkata 14 million Delhi 16.3 million Chennai 8.7 million Bangaluru 8.5 million	India has 39 cities with a population of more than 1 million.
Area	1,269,219 sq. miles (3,287,263 sq. km)	Seventh largest country in the world
Climate	It varies from tropical monsoon in the south to temperate in the north.	Best times to visit are October to March, or September through November if visiting the Himalayas.
Border Countries	Bangladesh, Bhutan, China, Myanmar, Nepal, Pakistan. There are 4,400 miles (7,000 km) of coastline.	Long-term border disputes with Pakistan
Government	Liberal democratic federal republic. Two houses of parliament: the upper Council of States (Rajya Sabha) and the lower House of the People (Lok Sabha)	The head of state, elected for a five-year term, is the President; the head of government is the Prime Minister. There are 29 states and 7 union territories.
Population	1.38 billion (2020). Second largest in the world	Plus 16 million in the Indian Diaspora
Age Structure	Population below 15 yrs, 26.9%; 15–24 yrs, 17.79%; 25 –54 yrs, 41%; below 65 yrs, 96.39%	

Life Expectancy	Male 67.8; female 70.5	
Ethnic Makeup	Indo-Aryan 72%; Dravidian 25%; Mongoloid and other 3%	
Religion	Hindus 79.8%; Muslims 14.2%; Christians 2.3%; Sikhs 1.7%; Buddhists 0.7%; Jains 0.4%; others 0.9%	
Languages	Hindi is the official language, spoken primarily in the north. There are 22 officially recognized languages and 1,950 other languages spoken.	English is recognized by the constitution as an associate national language.
Literacy	74.04%: males 81%; females 65%	Literacy among the young (15–24 yrs): 88.4% (m); 74.4% (f)
Gross Domestic Product	US $3.2 trillion (2020)	GNI per capita: US $2,338 (2020)
Per Capita Income	US $1,964	22% live below the poverty line.
Currency	Indian rupees (Rs.)	1USD = 73.75 IR (2020)
Electricity	230 volts, 50 Hz	Round-prong plug required. Frequent blackouts and load shedding
Video	PAL system	
Internet Domain	.in	
Telephone	India's country code is 91.	To dial out of India dial 00, followed by the oountry oodo.
Time	GMT + 5.5 hrs	No seasonal time change

CHAPTER ONE

LAND & PEOPLE

BOUNDARIES AND *BANDHAN*

Bounded by the Himalayas to the north, the Arabian Sea to the west, and the Bay of Bengal to the east, the immense peninsula of India sits on a separate tectonic plate from the rest of Asia, together with its neighbors, Pakistan and Bangladesh. It also shares borders with China, Nepal, Bhutan, and Myanmar (Burma).

Throughout history, outsiders have identified this vast country as a place set apart. The Greek historian Herodotus in the fifth century BCE first dubbed it "India," having heard of the land across the Indus or Sindhu River from Persian travelers. The Persians called it "Hindustan"—"land of the people of the Sindhu River." Mughal conquerors called the indigenous peoples "Hindus." "Hindustan" came into popular usage during the British Raj and is experiencing a resurgence today with the rise of Hindu fundamentalism. Within its borders the linguistic, ethnic, political, religious, and topographical differences are mind-boggling. Nagaland in the northeast boasts mahogany and rattan forests, and a Christian history. Off India's shores lie the sparsely inhabited coral atolls of the predominantly Muslim Lakshadweep, and the distinct peoples who live on the volcanic chain of the Andaman and Nicobar Islands.

In between you'll find climate and geographic extremes inhabited by thousands of peoples and linguistic groups with rich and varied traditions.

Despite this great diversity, Indians identify themselves as a single people—as Bharat. Found in the ancient texts of the *Rig Veda* and the *Bhagavad Gita*, as well as in ancient Tamil, the name "*Bharatam*" referred to the people of the Indian peninsula. Bound together by their history, a complex but common social structure, and shared cultural values, the people of the peninsula have developed a separate and strong identity. At Independence, "Bharat" was adopted as the official name of the new nation.

GEOGRAPHY AND CLIMATE

With the seventh-largest landmass in the world, India's geography ranges from the breathtaking Himalayas to scorching desert, to dense tropical forests, to expansive plains. Around 4,400 miles (7,000 km) of coast provide beautiful beaches, rocky cliffs, and marshlands. The Ganges River cuts through the dry northern plains to merge forces with Central and South Asia's major river, the Yamuna, before pouring out into the Bay of Bengal. Rivers and tributaries, mostly flowing from the

UNITED INDIA

Raksha Bandhan is a Hindu festival honoring the brother–sister relationship. On the day of the full moon in the Hindu month of Shravan, which falls in August, girls tie silk threads, or *rakhis* ("bonds of protection") on the wrists of brothers and those boys they see as brothers. *Rakhis* were used to demonstrate against partition and sectarian violence in Bengal in the run-up to Independence. Declaring to the British government that Bengal was "one and indivisible," people took an oath binding their lives together beyond the ties of blood and religious affiliation.

Himalayas, run through the subcontinent like veins. These waters bring both life and death to India. The Yamuna, a valuable waterway depositing enormous amounts of fertile soil, has also become a frequent source of flooding.

India can be divided into five geographical regions: the Islands, the Coastal Plains, the Peninsula Plateau, the North Plains, and the North Mountains. There are three major seasons—summer, monsoon, and winter—but climate changes with the geography. Tropical, subtropical, arid, and alpine zones can all be found within this vast subcontinent.

Kerala, in the southwest, is known as "the gateway of summer monsoon." But even Kerala's 111 inches

(282 cm) of average annual rainfall can't compare with
the northeast state of Meghalaya, which boasts the top
two wettest places in the world with annual rainfalls of
464–467 inches (1,178–1,187 cm).

Across the arid northwest plains, temperatures range
from 104 to 115ºF (40–46ºC), though they have been
known to rise to 140ºF (60ºC)In spite of scorching
temperatures and little rain in the arid regions of the
west in the summer months, these areas support a rich
variety of vegetation and animal life.

The Thar, or Great Indian Desert, covering much of
Rajasthan and parts of Gujarat, and the Himalayas in the
north, affect India's climate. Blocking the cold winds from
central Asia, the Himalayas guarantee warmer temperatures
than India would otherwise experience. The north is a
place of extremes: bone-chilling temperatures in winter
give way to the scorching Loo wind in summer, when life
is difficult for all who work or travel there. As June moves
into July and August, heat and humidity rise to unbearable
heights. A sigh of relief is heard when the monsoon finally
breaks, with often awe-inspiring thunderstorms, sheets of
rain, and overflowing rivers.

From September to November, the monsoons wane
in the west, drenching the east as winter approaches.

Winter in India, from December to February, is
relatively dry and cool. Temperatures are, on the average,
50–60ºF (10–15ºC). Southern regions are warmed by
the surrounding waters of the Indian Ocean, the Bay of
Bengal, and the Arabian Sea. Parts of India do see snow.
Himachal Pradesh, Uttarakhand, and Shimla, in the
north, are known for their ski resorts.

Ki monastery, a Buddhist monastery in Spiti Valley in Himachal Pradesh.

THE PEOPLE

At around 1.4 billion, India has the second-largest
population in the world. In the past forty years, it has
doubled. With 17.5 percent of the earth's population
and growing by one birth per second, it promises to
overtake China.

Though the urban population has multiplied
elevenfold during the last century, 70 percent of Indians
still live in villages. Migration to the cities continues
to rise due to loss of lands and crops caused by flood
and drought, coupled with a desire for better education
and work opportunities. But most rural migrants find

themselves joining the immense slum populations and living in absolute poverty. In 2017, India ranked 130th on the United Nations Human Development Index. It is estimated that nearly 500 million more people will move to the city by 2050. Cities of a million are considered towns in this country where its two major cities, Delhi and Mumbai, each boast numbers approaching twenty million.

Language and Literacy

India is a linguist's paradise, with more than 1,950 languages, including the two classical languages of Sanskrit and Tamil. There are more than twenty-two official languages, with Hindi and English as the official languages for government affairs and business.

Indians value education highly. According to the 2011 Annual Status of Education Report, 97 percent of rural children are enrolled in school, but there is a high degree of absenteeism and the dropout rate across the country is on the rise. India's literacy rate has continued to climb, from 12 percent at the end of British rule to more than 74 percent. But there is still a drastic difference between south India, which has mandatory government-funded education until the age of sixteen, and the north, which does not. The contrast is great, with parts of Kerala having 100 percent literacy contrasted with Bihar's 64 percent. And there are the expected, though diminishing, variations between urban (86 percent) and rural (71 percent), and between male (81 percent) and female (65 percent).

Religion

Close to 80 percent of the population are registered
as Hindus. Though only 14.2 percent of Indians are
Muslim, India has the third-largest Muslim population
in the world (the largest for a non-Muslim majority
country) and is projected to be the first by 2050. The
remainder is made up of Christians, mainly living in
the south and the northeast (2.3 percent), Sikhs
(1.7 percent), Buddhists (0.7 percent), and Jains
(0.4 percent). Jews, Zoroastrians, Baha'is, and others
comprise 0.9 percent.

The introduction of secularism in the last century
was not meant to erase or replace religion in this
profoundly spiritual country, but to win independence
from the British and promote the political unification
of culturally distinct kingdoms and peoples. But in this
century, the vision of a united India is being ripped
apart by increased religion-related tension.

A BRIEF HISTORY

Ancient Indus (c. 3300–1500 BCE)

India's ancient civilization was born in the Indus River
Valley, in the northwest region of the subcontinent,
and flourished during the Bronze Age. The people of
the valley, the Harappans, lived in multistoried brick
homes with sewers, wells, and trash chutes, in well-laid-
out towns. They developed metallurgical techniques to
produce bronze, lead, tin, and copper. Grain was the
currency of exchange and taxation.

Vedic Period (c. 1500–500 BCE)

It was in this valley that the Aryans first surfaced in
Indian history. It is still debated whether the "Noble
Ones," as they called themselves, migrated from Eurasia
or arose as the indigenous culture of the Indus Valley.
Whatever their origin, they settled in villages across
North India and the plains of the Ganges, establishing
the Vedic civilization. Essentially tribal, these semi-
nomadic people lived off the land, and introduced their
religious beliefs of multiple gods and goddesses who
were worshiped through fire and ritual.

The Aryans established absolute monarchies and
a hierarchy of nobility in the north. What became the
Hindu caste system originated during this period,
as kings assigned specific duties to individuals, who
passed these responsibilities on to their heirs. Soon
education and occupation were determined by birth.

As the Aryan kings occupied more territories, the
Dravidians, an indigenous population predating the
rise of the Aryans, were pushed south.

Many religious texts were created and passed on
during this era. The *Vedas* (Sanskrit, "knowledge"),
after which this period is named, laid the foundations
of Hinduism and other major features of Indian
culture.

The four *Vedas* took shape through oral tradition
from 1500 BCE and were codified in 600 BCE. The
philosophical *Upanishads*, the *Bhagavad-Gita*, and the
Mahabharata, the longest epic poem ever written, all
sprang from this period. The *Laws of Manu*, recorded
in Sanskrit, prescribes rules of life for Hindus and

solidified the castes into the four main strata that characterize India's social structure today.

In the fifth century BCE, a prince of the Shakya clan, Siddhartha Gautama, attained "Enlightenment," becoming known as the Buddha, or Enlightened One, and founded the religion of Buddhism. At the same time, Vardhamana Mahavira preached what was later to become Jainism.

As the sixteen Great Kingdoms, or *Maha Janapadas*, arose across the Indo-Gangetic plain, India experienced its second major period of urbanization.

Persian Empire (500–350 BCE)

The Persian king, Cyrus the Great, conquered India's northwestern region in 538 BCE. Eighteen years later, his son-in-law, Darius the Great (520 BCE), consolidated the rule of the Persians over the Indian subcontinent, lasting for the next two hundred years. Persian political systems influenced future forms of government adopted on the subcontinent.

Alexander the Great (327–323 BCE)

The conquering Macedonian king, Alexander the Great, crossed into India in 327 BCE to be welcomed by Ambhi, king of Taxila in western Punjab. At war with his eastern and northern neighbors, Ambhi hoped to enlist Alexander's aid against his enemies. Aid him he did, Alexander vanquished every tribe, confederation, and king on his quest to reach Asia.

Once they had reached the Beas River (a tributary of the Ganges), Alexander's exhausted and disgruntled troops pressed him to head home. Turning back just nineteen months after he had entered India, Alexander left deputies to govern the Indian provinces.

Two years after Alexander's death in 323 BCE, these governors abandoned their posts and divided his empire among themselves. But when Seleucus I Nicator (the Conqueror) decided to recover the lost Indian lands in 305 BCE, he found his way blocked by Chandragupta Maurya, an exiled and possibly illegitimate son of the Magadha royal family. As Chandragupta proved too powerful to defeat, Seleucus made an alliance with him.

The Great Mauryan Empire (322–185 BCE)

The Mauryan Empire, regarded as the greatest in Indian history, dominated the subcontinent during the fourth and third centuries BCE. Its founder, Chandragupta Maurya, united the Empire; his son, Bendusara, expanded it; and his grandson, Ashoka, made it great.

On learning of Alexander's death and the fragmentation of his empire, Chandragupta led a band of guerrillas in overthrowing King Dhama Nanda of Magadha in eastern India and slaughtering the royal family. He conquered the Northwest Frontier and most of Afghanistan, and created an empire that extended from the Bay of Bengal to the Arabian Sea and Persia. Chandragupta Maurya ruled for twenty-four years. His reign was not a benevolent one. This new emperor lived in such fear of assassination that he slept in a different room each night to confuse his enemies. He gave up his throne toward the end of his life and embraced Jainism. He was succeeded by his son, and then his grandson, Ashoka.

Ashoka the Great (273–232 BCE)

Ashoka the Great, born in 304 BCE, was emperor of all of the Indian subcontinent—or nearly all. His decision to extend his rule to the unconquered kingdom of Kalinga on the Bay of Bengal brought about a conversion of the man and his empire.

The carnage of war shook Ashoka. Turning to the teachings of Buddha, he set aside his weapons to put on the robes of a Buddhist monk.

This "Emperor of Emperors" effected reforms including the outlawing of animal sacrifice, the religious

A relief sculpture of Ashoka the Great flanked by his two queens, at the Buddhist *stupas* of Sanchi Stupa (a UNESCO World Heritage Site) in the state of Madhya Pradesh.

education of his people, and sending Buddhist missionaries to the Greeks and into the Near East. His impact on Indian history is such that India's national emblem, the Lion of Sarnath, and the wheel on the Indian flag, known as the Ashoka Chakra, were both taken from his reign.

Four Asiatic lions standing back-to-back top the Ashoka pillar at the Buddhist site of Sarnath.

Between the two great empires of Maurya and Gupta, India was ruled regionally. It was in this in-between time, around 52 CE, that the apostle Thomas is said to have visited India, planting the seeds of Indian Christianity.

The Golden Age of the Guptas (320–550 CE)

Chandragupta I founded the Gupta dynasty; but the Golden Age of India began when Chandragupta II rose to power fifty years later, providing a stability through military might that enabled science, art, literature, and religion to reach their zenith.

Scholars of the day included the astronomer Aryabhatta, who is said to have been the first to conceptualize "zero." The exchange of ideas and knowledge, especially religious, was actively sought with China through a kind of missionary exchange. The Gupta Empire was also politically open, developing diplomatic contacts in south Asia, Indonesia, Persia, Greece, and Rome. As religious, diplomatic, and trade relationships expanded, the culture of the Guptas spread.

As is the fate of all great empires, the Gupta Empire weakened. When the Huns from Central Asia attacked in 450 CE, it could not hold them back. After the death of the last Gupta, Bhanugupta, in 570, the Empire collapsed. Once again India was ruled by smaller kingdoms and remained divided until the Muslim invasions in 1000.

The Classical Age of the North and South Kingdoms (647–1200)

Different empires dominated north and south, and were frequently at war with each other. Although three dynasties, known as the Rajputs, fought for control of the north, art and the religions of Hinduism, Buddhism, and Jainism still flourished during the Classical Age.

Another culture was growing in the rich soil of the south, developing an art, literature, and architecture distinctly its own. The Dravidians, driven south by the Aryans long ago, now ruled kingdoms in the southern regions and expanded vast overseas empires in Southeast Asia. They traded spices with the Roman Empire and Southeast Asia. The sciences and mathematics, as well as religion and philosophy, developed under the rule of these kings.

The Delhi Sultanate and the Beginning of Colonization (1200–1500)

For centuries Muslims from the north and west had made their way to India. Some came for riches, others to spread Islam; but most noted in history are those who came to rule. In a pattern that became familiar to India, Muslim traders arrived before Muslim invaders.

Delhi was captured in 1192 from the Rajput Hindu king Prithvi Raj Chauhan by Muhammed of Ghor, a Muslim general from what is today Afghanistan. Ghor founded the first of a series of dynasties to rule as the Delhi Sultanate.

During the reign of the Delhi Sultans many north Indian Hindus and Buddhists converted to Islam. The Sultans eventually controlled much of south India as well. In 1351 the south regained its independence as a Hindu state. Central India, too, rebelled, becoming a separate, though still Islamic, state. The Delhi Sultanate ended with the Mongol invasion of Timur in 1398.

Seafaring explorers from China and Europe made their way to India. The Portuguese explorer Vasco da Gama was commissioned to find a sea route to India in 1497. Soon after, the Portuguese, Dutch, British, and French had set up trading posts on India's west coast.

These traders turned the rivalry of the warring kingdoms to their advantage, setting up not only trading posts but also political stakes across the land. By the end of the Delhi Sultanate era, the British had acquired all the European colonized territories in India except for French Pondicherry and Chandernagore, Dutch Tranvancore, and Portuguese Goa, Daman, and Diu.

The Great Mughal Empire (1526–1761)
In 1526, local Indian nobles, angered by Ibrahim Shah Lodi, the Sultan of Delhi, took revenge by inviting the Uzbek descendant of Genghis Khan, Zahir ud-din

Muhammad Babur, ruler of Kabul, to invade Delhi and
Agra. These nobles unwittingly helped Babur to usher
in the Islamic Mughal Empire that would rule northern
India for two hundred years.

Akbar the Great (1542–1605)

Jalaluddin Muhammad Akbar, known as Akbar the
Great, ascended the throne when he was only thirteen
years old. This grandson of Babur, seeking tolerance
and peace, created new alliances and put an end to
laws that penalized non-Muslims. Akbar was so serious
about spiritual matters that he formed his own syncretic
religion, *Din-i-ilahi* ("Divine Faith").

A great patron of the arts, Akbar enlarged the
collections of Mughal art and literature. North Indian
art and architecture were transformed as the Mughals

The Masjid-i Jahān-Numā (the World-reflecting Mosque) in Delhi.

built palaces, forts, and monumental tombs. Shah Jahan, most famous for his architectural wonders of the Red Fort, Jama Masjid, and the Taj Mahal, was Akbar's grandson. The Mughal Empire declined following the death of Shah Jehan's son Aurangzeb, whose reign is the subject of political controversy today. He reinstated the poll tax on non-Muslims that had been abolished by Akbar, and destroyed important Hindu temples such as Vrindavan, Somnath, and Kashi Vishwanath. Aurangzeb is regarded by some modern scholars as being fundamentally anti-Hindu; others view the demolition of temples as a strategic part of the military campaign to preserve the unity of his restless realm.

Power was once again decentralized as lesser kingdoms unsuccessfully sought to replace the Mughals. When the British government took control of India from the East India Company in 1858, more than one hundred kings were found to be issuing coins as the "Mughal Emperor."

The East India Company and Colonial India (1600–1947)

The East India Company was granted a charter by Queen Elizabeth I of England in 1600 with the aim of securing exclusive trading rights with India. The Mughal emperor Jahangir led the way in opening India's door to the Company in 1617. Sixty years later, when Siraj-ud-Doula, the Nawab of Bengal, refused to follow suit, the Company formed a private army, led by Robert Clive, and defeated the Nawab and his French allies. Clive was appointed as the East India Company's first Governor of Bengal in 1757. The Company created a trade monopoly in Bengal, introducing the Permanent Settlement, a land taxation system set up on a feudal-like structure. From 1772 to 1785 Warren Hastings, the Governor General of Bengal, raised a native army and pursued expansionist policies. By 1818 the Company controlled most of India.

Growing discontent with British rule among the sepoys—Hindu and Muslim soldiers serving in the Company's three armies—culminated in open rebellion in 1857 (the "Indian Mutiny"). The insurgents called on the emperor in Delhi to lead them. The British eventually captured Delhi and conquered all the rebel strongholds. Bahadur Shah Zafar, the last of the Mughal emperors, who led this "First War of Independence," was exiled to Burma and his family line was extinguished. The British Crown now took direct control of India, the greatest of its colonies.

The British Raj ("reign") lasted from 1858 to 1947. It included areas directly administered by Britain and semiautonomous princely states ruled by Indian rulers under the ultimate authority of the British Crown.

During the nineteenth century, the British developed the country's economic, legal, and educational infrastructure, but skewed the economy to serve their own interests. Imperial rule was a mixture of paternalism and racism, and in 1885 the Indian National Congress was founded in Bombay to counter the more repressive aspects of the Raj. By the 1940s India's huge contribution of troops and treasure to Great Britain's war effort, in both World Wars, had changed the way Indians perceived their situation

The Indian Independence Movement (1940s)

Mohandas Karamchand Gandhi (1869–1948), who became known as the "Father of India," was one of many

who sought India's independence from the British.
At first the *Mahatma* ("Great Soul") campaigned
for equality and civil rights within the Raj, until it
became clear that his ideals could not be realized
unless there were freedom from foreign domination.
He joined together with other, passionate leaders such
as Jawaharlal Nehru, secretary of the Indian National
Congress, to create a national movement that would
roll over India like a wave, pushing the British out by
the power of mass nonviolent action.

The revolution that began to brew in the 1920s was
not wholly nonviolent. Subash Chandra Bose broke away
from Congress and during the Second World War, with
Japanese help, organized the anti-British Indian National
Army. The executed young revolutionary Bhagat Singh

Mohandas Karamchand Gandhi in conversation with Jawaharlal Nehru during
a meeting of the All India Congress in Bombay, July 6, 1946.

became a celebrated Indian martyr. These and many other great and small men and women fanned the flames of the freedom movement that culminated in India's independence in 1947.

Bharat's Birth Pangs (1948–1991)

No longer able to sustain its rule over India, Britain made a virtue of necessity and conceded its independence. In 1946 elections were called, in which the Congress Party won eight of the eleven provinces. But now the history of conflict between Muslims and Hindus on the subcontinent raised its head as the Muslim minority feared rule by a Hindu government. Intercommunal violence broke out. The Muslim League, led by Muhammad Ali Jinnah, called for an independent Muslim state. Partition, or separation of Pakistan from India, was Britain's parting gift.

The last British Viceroy, Lord Louis Mountbatten, speeded up the process with the imposition of a deadline for partition. On August 15, 1947, India became a sovereign state, and Pakistan was created from the Muslim majority areas. Twelve million Muslims, Hindus, and Sikhs began the largest migration in modern history, uprooting families and leaving properties to move to what they hoped would be a safe land ruled by their own people. The riots that broke out during the exodus left half a million dead.

Another shock wave hit the country when, on January 30, 1948, Gandhi, who had opposed partition, was assassinated by a young Hindu nationalist, angered by his call for a united India for Muslims and Hindus.

Jawaharlal Nehru was the first prime minister of the new self-governing democracy. He was succeeded by

Lal Bahadur Shastri, who faced ongoing conflict with Pakistan over Indian-held Kashmir, which culminated in the Indo–Pakistan War of 1965, after which he met with Pakistan's president to sign a peace declaration.

Following Shastri's death in 1966, Nehru's daughter, Indira Gandhi, became prime minister. She presided over India's victory in the second Indo–Pakistani War, which resulted in the establishment of Bangladesh, formerly East Pakistan, as a separate nation, in 1971.

Another bomb burst when Mrs. Gandhi was found guilty of electoral fraud in 1975. Her response was to declare a state of emergency and impose authoritarian rule for nineteen months. She imprisoned a thousand political opponents and began a mandatory birth-control program to sterilize the mentally retarded and large populations of villagers, resulting in more than seven million vasectomies.

Not surprisingly, Mrs. Gandhi's government lost the election following the state of emergency, but she returned to power three years later. In 1984, Indira Gandhi was assassinated by her Sikh bodyguards in retaliation for the government's attack on the Sikhs' Golden Temple.

In the tradition of India's great dynasties, Rajiv Gandhi, her second son, immediately, if reluctantly, took his mother's place. Accused of corruption, his government collapsed in 1989. While running for election in 1991, Rajiv's last act was to greet a young woman who had seemingly come to touch his feet. The bomb blast from that suicide bomber, a Tamil Tiger sympathizer, left India reeling.

Bharat the Great (1991–present)

The new millennium is witnessing a great transformation in the culture and global influence of Bharat. India has become an economic powerhouse in the world economy. During the early 1990s, extensive financial reforms were made by the finance minister, Manmohan Singh, leading to rapid economic growth.

Singh became known as the Father of Indian Economic Reform and went on to be elected prime minister in 2004 and again in 2009. He reduced government deficits, launched large-scale rural job programs, provided debt relief to farmers, and created economic policies and tax reforms that changed the economic climate.

India has also become a nuclear power. In 2006, it signed a nuclear agreement with the US, giving it access to civilian nuclear technology, American expertise, and nuclear fuel, with India promising to separate civilian and military nuclear programs and be subject to permanent international inspections. Two years later, the US began nuclear trade with India; and in 2009, Russia agreed to supply India with US $700 million worth of uranium. Today nuclear power is India's fifth-largest source of electricity.

GOVERNMENT AND POLITICS

India is the world's largest democracy. A republic, it consists of twenty-nine states and seven union territories and the New Capital Territory of Delhi. Historically the central government has had greater sway than the states;

but the political, economic, and social reforms of the 1990s have increased the power of the states.

The Executive branch consists of the president, the vice president, and the Council of Ministers, headed by the prime minister. The president, as head of state, is elected for a five-year term by an electoral college. The prime minister is appointed by the president and is subordinate to the legislative branch of the lower house of parliament.

The Legislature consists of two houses of parliament: the upper Rajya Sabha (States Council) and the lower Lok Sabha (People's House). Rajya Sahba members are elected by states for a six-year term. Lok Sabha members are elected by the popular vote of individual constituencies and serve a five-year term.

The Judiciary is headed by a Chief Justice, and includes twenty-one High Courts and the Supreme Court. The Supreme Court has the power to make laws and to overturn laws made by states that it deems to be unconstitutional.

Political parties in India are as numerous as Hindu gods, with dozens of state-recognized and well over one thousand unrecognized regional parties competing for election. States have their own governments. When a party is recognized by four states, it becomes a national party. In 2019 there were seven national parties.

Despite the complexities of Indian politics and the variance in levels of education, every Indian can explain how their government works and give an opinion about current affairs. Newspapers, radio, television, and the Internet are part of everyday life.

They are all vital sources of global political information. For Indians, talking politics is like breathing.

Indians are passionate about their politics and dumbfounded by anyone who is not. The zeal and power seen in India's political history is still visible today in spontaneous political rallies that often combust into violent riots and in the high turnout at voting polls. Since Mahatma Gandhi's famous near-death fasts to bring attention to the plight of outcastes or to stop violent conflicts, many Indians have been willing to sacrifice their lives in an effort to persuade those who have the power to effect change.

THE ECONOMY

For four decades India's economic growth was stunted by ideologically inspired policy restrictions and political corruption. Attempts to embrace aspects of capitalism while holding on to Nehru's socialism failed to bring the hoped-for social and economic results. When the Soviet Union, India's major trading partner, collapsed and the Gulf War caused oil prices to skyrocket, India faced a financial crisis of bailout proportions.

Manmohan Singh's reforms catapulted India into becoming the world's fastest-growing economy. GDP continued to grow throughout the world recession of 2008–09. In fact, the IT sector grew 20 percent that year.

When Narendra Modi came into power in 2014, he aspired to bring in a new day in India's economy. In 2015, Modi's government made visas available upon arrival for the first time in ongoing efforts to boost the economy through tourism, as well as business. And he has taken other giant steps to bring economic change, not all of it successful: 86 percent of India's cash was demonetized, making it worthless overnight, and there have been confusing new tax reforms and restrictive new labor laws. Rising Hindu nationalism is also contributing to the changing shape of business.

In spite of seeming setbacks, India's economy continues to grow, due in part to the fact that 18 percent of its GDP and 50 percent of its workforce is still based on agriculture. For centuries India has been known for its exports. "Made in India" received a boost in a 2009 policy aimed at doubling India's export of goods and services. Prime Minister Modi launched a "Make in India" initiative early in his tenure, enticing foreign business into India. In his first year, the number of Japanese companies in India rose by 15 percent.

India has also produced brilliant innovations in computer engineering and marketing. Indian-based technical support and software development is commonplace among the big boys of technology, from IBM and Apple to Coca-Cola and Pepsi. Indian service-provider companies are shifting from serving major companies to competing with them.

The New Middle Classes

Inside and outside the country, India's under-forties look much like any middle-class Westerners. India's middle class has doubled in recent years, and includes not only educated professionals, but "blue collar" workers such as vendors, carpenters, and electricians. In contrast to previous generations, today's middle class invests less in land and gold, choosing instead to buy a different kind of lifestyle. Choice and convenience increasingly determine how discretionary income is spent. As dual-income couples have become the norm in the city, so have supermarkets, packaged food, and a plethora of restaurant options. Cars that were once status symbols are now affordable by lower-middle-class families. However, in contrast to visible signs of growing wealth, Indians feel they are going backward. In a recent Gallup poll, only 3 percent of the population felt that they were "thriving" economically, compared to 14 percent in 2014.

Highly-educated Indians, with entrepreneurial vision and motivation, continue to market themselves globally. There are 31 million non-resident Indians throughout the world who are sending US $70 billion back home.

It's not only money that's making its way back home. Indians who once moved to the West to find work and wealth are returning to India. The shortage of IT professionals, engineers, and managers today means greater opportunity for employment and advancement inside India. The move "back home" has been driven by factors such as the cost of living, social and education concerns for children, family support, and the Overseas Citizen of India (OCI) options for those with US and other passports. The shift in India's economy and the openness to entrepreneurs makes the grass look greener on the South Asian side of the fence. India will soon become the world's fastest-growing economy. Yet bleak poverty still plagues this country.

India is experiencing an epidemic of suicides among its farmers who struggle with debt and crop failure, attributable to rising temperatures.

The Widening Divide

Average wages in India doubled in a recent eighteen-year period. But that is not saying much when the per capita income is only US $2,338 and 224 million people in India live on less than US $1.90 per day. India has the highest concentration of poor on the planet, a fact made all the more dismal by the statistics related to children: it has the highest malnutrition rate of young children, with 39 percent of those under the age of three.

The labor force is second only to China in size. Sixty-four percent of the population is of working age and half of India's 1.4 billion are under the age of

Distinctive modern architecture dominates Bangalore's business zone.

twenty-five. Between 1991 and 2013, 300 million came
of working age, but only 140 million were employed.
This number will continue to skyrocket, with 280 million
more entering the job market by 2050. Many live without
the means to feed their families, much less educate
their children. Tens of thousands of men and women,
mostly unskilled laborers, are duped by promises of good
jobs abroad, only to discover when they reach their
destination that they are effectively enslaved. India's
chronic social challenges could sabotage all promise of
prosperity in the future. Yet the abundance of natural
resources and the resourcefulness of India's people
should not be underestimated.

CHAPTER TWO

VALUES & ATTITUDES

A SENSE OF IDENTITY

Indians have a passionate sense of belonging. One could categorize this as nationalism, and sometimes it is, but these feelings are not primarily about India as a political entity. Indian identity is fashioned by history, community, and family. The subcategories and subcultures of language, caste, state, and religion *are* India.

The answer to the question "Who am I?" goes much deeper than "I am an Indian," and far broader than "I am me." Indians define themselves by history ("I am an Anglo-Indian"); by religion ("I am a Sikh"); caste ("I am a Nadar"); people group ("I am Assamese"); state ("I am Tamilian"); language ("I am a Malayalee"); or any number of categories that may not exist in other cultures. To attempt to paint them with a single brush would be to fail to grasp their extraordinary complexity.

There are, however, shared values that transcend these divisions, giving Indians a common culture and enabling all to say together, "I am Indian."

HIERARCHY

Hierarchy is inescapable in India. Everything and everyone is ranked, up or down, from everything and everyone else. Your place in the social order determines how others treat you and what is expected of you.

Look at where people sit. Chairs are offered to people of consequence. Though this does not apply in urban settings where people congregate, such as in a restaurant, it is not unusual to enter a room and see a few "big men" seated on the available chairs and everybody else sitting on the floor. You may not be able to tell the difference between "high" and "low," but they can.

This is true within families, too. Language illustrates family hierarchy, structured according to age and gender. In many contexts, a wife does not address her husband by name, as an equal, but may refer to him as "Daddy," or another relational term. Children address older siblings using specific suffixes, as in Tamil's "*Annan*," elder brother, or Hindi's "*Didi*," big sister. From birth Indians learn who they are in the pecking order of family, community, and society. Outside the family, hierarchy in the community is often acknowledged using respectful familial titles, such as "*Bhai*," brother, in north India, or the English terms "Aunty" or "Uncle."

Caste

"Caste" was originally a Hindu concept, referring to the distinct hereditary groups ranked in the social order. Theologically, the four original castes, or *varnas*, sprang from the body of the creator god, Brahma: Brahmins or priests from the mouth, Kshatriyas or rulers from the arms, Vaishyas, merchants and farmers, from the thighs, and Shudras, the artisans and servants, from the feet. Initially based on occupation, these *varnas* are now rigid categories dictating value and life possibilities not just for Hindus, but for all Indians.

Each finger should have its own width.
Tamil proverb

Caste groups are too numerous to name. Thousands of castes and subcastes are found across India. Regional and religious subcultures have their own discernible caste delineations. A person's name, birthplace, and physical features can be indicators of caste.

Some people will tell you that caste has been abolished, and that's true on paper. There have been significant improvements in educational and vocational opportunity for "lower castes" and "outcastes." (Though to take advantage of those opportunities, official forms must record your caste.) In urban settings, caste appears to matter less. On jam-packed buses you don't know who you're rubbing shoulders with. In busy restaurants you have no control over who cooks your food or who sits at the next table. On the street people do not wear caste badges or the clothing that once signified one's caste. Many Indians have modified their names to make their caste unrecognizable. In these contexts, class distinction, based on education and income, becomes predominant.

But caste consciousness is alive and well. Indians seem to have a radar born of personal and cultural history, scanning for clues that indicate where they fit in the puzzle that is the caste system. Even for those who are less observant of caste protocols in daily life, when important life decisions such as marriage must be made, the importance of caste becomes very evident.

There are those who live outside caste. The 16.6 percent of the population who are too low to be considered part of the caste system are called, variously, "Dalit," "Untouchable," "Harijan," and "Scheduled." In the 1950s Dr. B. R. Ambedkar, a Dalit political leader, converted from Hinduism to Buddhism in protest against the caste system.

Millions have subsequently followed his example, converting to Buddhism or Christianity to escape the clutches of caste. Though, theologically, Buddhists believe all distinctions to be unreal, and Christians affirm the unity of all believers, in real life caste is present in all India's religions. Not allowed to be truly out of caste, the Dalits have in effect become a fifth caste, demonstrating the hold of the system.

Class

Class is linked to caste. There are three main classes: forward (higher castes), backward (middle and lower castes), and Dalit. Class often forms the basis of political groups and alliances. There is a general correlation between caste and prosperity: the higher the caste, the more options the individuals have had for education, connection, and advancement.

Whoever owns the stick owns the buffalo.
Hindi proverb

The National Council of Applied Economic Research defines "middle class" as those who have a purchasing power of US $10 per day. By this definition, 50 percent of India's population is "middle class."

One unforeseen outcome of becoming middle class has been the tension between communal and individual identity and fulfillment. A dutiful son might have bought his parents a car, or provided for the education of young cousins. But now, living in a different city or even another country, with a greater amount of expendable income, who's to know if he spends that money on a Harley and his latest girlfriend?

The middle class consists of self-made men and women. But their road to prosperity is not one that all Indians can travel. Although the government has poured money into higher education since Independence, most Indians have not been educated to university entrance level. Most are too poor and too distanced from the education and social networks that lead to decent jobs to rise along with them. In recent decades, quota requirements in education and government have made it possible for some in the "backward" class to begin the economic climb, but ancient hierarchies and ongoing discrimination make the climb a difficult one.

Many in the middle class are using their power not only to meet the needs of their extended family, but to care for the poor. Small nonprofit organizations focused on meeting the needs of women and children have sprung up all over India. But it may be difficult for the middle class to see itself as a unique "class," since caste and religion are the key defining cultural categories.

Foreigners and Hierarchy

In India, don't expect to find what Westerners regard as fairness or equality. These are not values that Indians see as necessary or even good.

In the West, we also have hierarchies built on class, personal and political history, and family-taught prejudices. But for most of us, these demarcations are permeable and can be overcome by effort or changed over time. That is alien to the Indian concept of hierarchy. One's role in the community and family, one's identity, educational and vocational options, and appropriate life connections are all determined by the caste and family into which one is born.

Respect is considered a fundamental right of those who were born "above." To disrespect (by disobeying or disregarding) someone above you is serious enough to bring shame, disgrace, and social punishment not only on you, but on your family and all those connected to you.

This difference in values may cause the visitor to experience a degree of internal, if not external, conflict. But hierarchy can sometimes work to your advantage as a foreigner. Caucasian men are shown respect as someone "above" on the social scale. This is especially true if you are "the boss." White women, too, seem to be in a special category, given access, privilege, and respect often withheld from Indian women.

This does not apply to all foreigners. As in many places in the world, discrimination and sometimes ill-treatment come according to pigmentation. Darker-hued people from anywhere, be it India, Africa, or Europe, will find themselves at the bottom of the social pecking order. People from neighboring countries come up against old prejudices and long-held stereotypes, born of fear of China to the north, or tied to the Tamil–Sinhala conflict in the south. Pakistan and India suffer from more than seventy years of bloodshed, war, and bad attitudes on both sides.

RELIGION

Despite differences in theology, history, and practice, Indians typically believe that religion is crucial to one's identity and to the well-being of family and society.

> **Worship without devotion is a**
> **waste of ritual leaves.**
> *Telugu proverb*

Hinduism

Hindus make up almost 80 percent of India's population. Ask ten Hindus to describe their religion, and you may get ten related but not identical answers. Hinduism is a relatively recent formulation of a belief system that developed over millennia. Philosophically, Hinduism is pantheistic monism, essentially the belief that "All is One, One is All, All is God." There is one undifferentiated, impersonal divine consciousness, Brahman, which is the only Reality. Everything else is *maya*, or illusion.

The purpose of the Hindu sacred texts is to illuminate the truth that All is One, lighting the way to escape the illusory cycle of death and rebirth, returning to the One. Hinduism as it is practiced is a religion of story, focusing on ideology and ritual. Many of its sacred writings tell stories about *avatars*—gods and goddesses that are manifestations of Brahman's descent from the metaphysical to the physical, and the most visible part of Hinduism. Though they are merely mirages of the truth, the worship of these deities is seen by all but the intellectual elite as an essential part of Hinduism.

Hindu philosophy is complex and a matter of debate for intellectuals; but to most Hindus it is simply a way

Devotees performing the *arati* ritual with incense smoke at a *ghat* on the Ganges River in the holy city of Varanasi.

of life. While Hinduism does not have a single unifying holy text, historical leader, or statement of beliefs, there are clearly recognized core beliefs and practices.

Dharma, or duty, sometimes translated as "truth," calls individuals to fulfil their responsibilities within their families and communities by wholeheartedly doing what they were born to do.

Samsara is the cycle of birth, life, death, and rebirth that is the destiny of every living thing. The traditional Hindu insistence on a vegetarian diet is the logical conclusion of this belief in reincarnation.

Karma, the moral law of cause and effect, determines the status of rebirth. Do your duty and it will be better for you next time. Do good and good will happen to you in the next life. Your eventual escape from rebirth, or *moksha*, is determined by your actions in your present life.

Puja, prasad, and *tilak* are tangible signs of devotion. Wives and mothers, who are responsible for the spiritual well-being of their husbands and children, perform rituals (*puja*) in the home at the shrine of the family deity, first offering flowers, food, or fire to the god, then *prasad* to their families. *Prasad*, the food offered to the god, is usually *ladoo* (sweet nut and chickpea balls). Purified by prayers and rituals, this holy food carries a blessing from the deity to anyone who eats it.

Pujas performed by priests in the temples confer blessings, forgiveness, or spiritual power to those who go there with offerings of money or food. Hindu worshipers scoop up blessing from the fire that is offered by the priests, sweeping their hands from the flame to their face or the top of their head. Those who have performed the *puja* mark the forehead of the blessed with ash from the fire or from a powder made of turmeric, saffron, clay, or vermilion. Often the shape of the *tilak* indicates the deity worshiped.

What foreigners often take to be the worship of cows is rather a taboo against killing them. Cows have long been protected for social, religious, and practical reasons: they provide life through their milk; they have a prominent place in the stories of Lord Krishna; and at one point in history they were synonymous with high-caste Brahmins.

Islam

Though Islam was introduced to India by conquest, it has become the faith of more than 14 percent of the population. From minarets all over India, Muslims are called to prayer five times a day with the declaration: "There is no god but Allah, and Muhammad is his Prophet." For Muslims, religion guides their lives, beginning with the call to prayer whispered in a baby's ear before he or she is named and ending with recitations from the Koran over the grave.

Founded in Arabia in c. 622, Islam is based on the teachings of the Prophet Muhammad. Allah alone is Creator and Judge. Many Hebrew and Christian prophets are honored in Islam, but Muhammad, is regarded as "the Seal of the Prophets."

The goal of Islam, meaning "submission," is to do good and shun evil in order to please Allah (God) and by His mercy enter into Paradise. This commitment is expressed through the Five Pillars.

THE FIVE PILLARS OF ISLAM

Shahada: profession of the faith

Salat: praying five times a day

Zakat: almsgiving to the poor

Sawm: self-purification through fasting during the month of Ramadan (when the revelation was given to Muhammad)

Hajj: undertaking the *hajj*, the pilgrimage to Mecca, at least once in one's lifetime

Because Islam is strictly monotheistic, idols are anathema. The physical representation of the human form, even as art, is expressly forbidden. The Prophet, though revered, is not worshiped.

The word of God, revealed to the Prophet Muhammad by the Angel Gabriel, recited by him, and later written down, is recorded in the Koran. At home as well as in the mosque, copies of the Koran are placed on a stand, never on the floor or near anyone's feet. To disrespect it is to disrespect God and His prophet. The Koran has been translated, but for Muslims the true revelation is that given to Muhammad—in Arabic.

Indian Muslims, primarily Sunnis, also have distinct practices that are more Indian than Islamic. Sufis, Muslim mystics, came to India in the fourteenth century, spreading Islam through holy men who blended well into the pattern of Hindu gurus. These *pirs*, or living saints, gathered a following while they lived. After death, stories of their holy lives drew people to their tombs, which soon became places of prayer. As tales were told of miraculous cures, the tombs themselves became holy places. Today there are hundreds of *dargahs,* or "portals," to be found all over India. In passing, they might be mistaken for Hindu or Catholic shrines, were it not for the distinctive dress of the worshipers: streams of white-capped men reaching out to touch the tomb as they pray; clusters of black-robed women tying red threads around iron bars surrounding the holy site.

Christianity

Christianity reached India with Thomas, one of the twelve apostles who followed Jesus. The Malankara Mar Thoma Syrian Church of Kerala traces its roots directly to Thomas, who landed on the Malabar Coast in 52 CE. Though Christianity has been in India for two thousand years, missionaries have, in the last few centuries, contributed not only to the growth of Christianity in India, but also to the development of education and literacy, and to health and medicine.

Officially, Christians make up 2.3 percent of India's population. Living mainly in the south and the northeast, 60 percent are Roman Catholic. The largest Indian Protestant Church, the Church of South India, was created in 1947 when Presbyterians, Congregationalists, Methodists, and Anglicans united. Despite sharing a common creed, Indian Christians are divided by details of doctrine and also by the plague of caste. Whether Baptist or Catholic, Jacobite or Church of North India, all are caste-based communities perpetuated by birth, strong social identity, and strict taboos against marriage outside the community.

Forms of worship are varied. Some gather in large buildings with stained glass windows to sing hymns from books that have been translated from English; others meet in homes and sit on mats on the floor, singing *bhajans* (religious songs).

Buddhism

Though Buddhists are a tiny minority of eight million adherents, Buddhism originated in India and plays an important role in its history and culture. The founder of Buddhism, Siddhartha Gautama, was born a high-caste Hindu in the hills of Nepal in 563 BCE. Abandoning his comfortable life at the age of twenty-nine, he embarked on a search for meaning, first through fasting and asceticism and then through meditation. While traveling through Bihar, in northern India, Siddhartha determined to remain under a tree until he understood the reason for living. It was there that he attained enlightenment and understood the Four Noble Truths.

THE FOUR NOBLE TRUTHS
Suffering is universal.
Suffering is caused by desire.
Suffering can be prevented.
Suffering is overcome when desire is overcome.

Statue of Buddha near Belum Caves in Andhra Pradesh.

Having become "The Awakened One" (Buddha), Siddhartha gathered a band of disciples and created a monastic order that continues today.

There are two primary Buddhist tenets. The law of causation teaches that nothing happens by chance, but is based on *karma*. The law of impermanence teaches that everything changes. Nothing is destroyed, but simply returns in a different form, including the human soul through reincarnation.

The aim of Buddhism is to escape suffering and the cycle of rebirth by overcoming all desire and attaining enlightenment. Buddha's prescribed means of reaching enlightenment was by the Middle Way, spurning both excess and asceticism, and through the Eightfold Path of right view, thought, speech, action, livelihood, effort, mindfulness, and concentration.

Buddhism is philosophically a religion without a god, but the Buddha has become an object of worship for most of India's Buddhists. His statues and shrines can be found all across the subcontinent; the three holiest sites in India are Bodhgaya, Bihar, where he attained enlightenment; Sarnath, where he preached his first sermon, establishing Buddhism by "setting in motion the wheel of truth;" and Kushinagar, where he died.

Sikhism

Guru Nanak, the founder of Sikhism, was born in
1469 to a high-caste Hindu family. He was inspired by
the monotheism of Islam, and drawn to both Hindu
and Muslim saints. His preaching of the unification of
Hinduism and Islam attracted disciples ("*Sikhs*"). Guru
Nanak's teachings, which included Hindu and Muslim
holy texts, were eventually written down in the sacred
book, *Siri Guru Granth Sahib*.

It is the presence of the *Siri Guru Granth Sahib* that, for
Sikhs, makes a place holy. Many Sikh homes today have
a room or a space set apart for the holy book. This Sikh
sacred scripture continued to be developed by later Gurus.

Guru Arjun, the Fifth Guru, built the Golden Temple
at Amritsar. It was from there that he judged civil affairs,
establishing a tradition of a religious state. The Tenth
Guru, Govind Singh, trained Sikhs in military combat

Sikh pilgrim at the Hamandir Sahib (Golden Temple) in Amritsar.

to equip them to defend their faith. Guru Govind Singh, who died in 1708, was the last living Sikh Guru. Having created a collective body of initiates known as the *Khalsa*, or Pure Ones, he declared the end of the succession of human gurus and identified the sacred text as Guru for Sikhs in subsequent generations.

The brotherhood of the *Khalsa* are recognized by the five Ks: *Kesh* (uncut hair); *Kangha* (a wooden or ivory comb as a symbol of purity); *Kara* (a steel bracelet as a sign of determination); *Kripan* (a sword to defend the weak); and *Kuchha* (shorts, symbolizing alertness). At initiation, *Khalsa* Sikhs take on a new name: men become *Singh* (Lion) and women become *Kaur* (Princess).

Today 1.7 percent of Indians are Sikhs, with most living in the Punjab. They have been held together by a common culture, as well as by the core beliefs that God is one and that all men are equal. Rejecting the notions of a priesthood or organized decision-making body, local Sikh communities make decisions together based on the *Siri Guru Granth Sahib*. Attempts, like the one in early 2010, to create a new sect or detour from historical and communally held doctrines are met with censure by leaders and the broader community.

The Hindu belief in *karma* and reincarnation is part of Sikhism. Many Hindu life-cycle rituals, including cremation and the reading of Hindu scriptures, are part of the life of the Sikh. Because of the syncretistic nature of the religion, intermarriage with Hindus is common.

Sikh temples, or *gurdwaras* ("doorways to the Guru"), can be recognized by the Sikh flag flying overhead. These gathering places are centers for worship, religious education, and community service. Look inside and you'll see rows of men, women, and children eating a meal in huge halls where food is served endlessly. Opposing the Hindu caste system, Guru Nanak set up congregations of followers who shared a communal *langar* (kitchen) and meals, thus breaking down caste barriers.

Jainism

India's four million Jains, living primarily in Maharashtra and Rajasthan, trace their religion through twenty-four *Jinas* ("those who overcome"). The last of the *Jinas*, Vardhamana, or Mahavira ("The Great Hero"), was born to a ruling family in Bihar in the sixth century BCE. To find purification of conscience and the meaning of existence, Mahavira cast off his riches and began what became an austere quest for truth. He is said to have foresworn clothing and shelter, and eventually formed a monastic order, training others to find purity and enlightenment through asceticism. After many years, satisfied that he had fulfilled his purpose, Mahavira fasted until he died.

Karma is the foundation of Jainism. Believing that the soul is made pure by right conduct, faith, and knowledge, Jains conquer worldly desire through abstinence and asceticism, and follow a life of nonviolence (*ahimsa*). So that they do not inadvertently kill insects while breathing or walking, Jain monks and serious devotees cover their nose and mouth with a mask and clear their paths with small brooms. Inactivity cleanses one of desire and action, reversing the impact of past action. For the Jain, worship and other religious ritual is not focused on a Being, but the recognition of the ability of those in the past to overcome *karma* and extinguish the self.

"Sky-clad" Jains (*Digambaras*) live as Mahavira lived, within monasteries and without clothes. The few females that claim to be *Digambaras* must don robes. This virtually all-male sect teaches that women cannot be true monks or attain *moksha* (liberation) until they are reincarnated as men. "White-clad" Jains (*Deravasi*) wear white robes and mouth coverings. Both groups are divided by theological debate.

The holiest Jain shrine, carved in 981 BCE, stands on a hill outside Bangaluru, Karnataka. Every twelve years Jains come to anoint this vast statue of Gomateshvara, also known as *Bhagwan* ("lord" or god) Bahubali, with milk, ghee (clarified butter), and saffron. This giant is believed by Jains to be the first human being ever to attain enlightenment, thus becoming the first *Jina*.

Zoroastrianism

Most of India's one hundred thousand Zoroastrians live in Mumbai, in Maharashtra, and the rest live in Gujarat, where the first Zoroastrians arrived from Persia in the tenth century.

Zarathustra, or Zoroaster, is thought to have founded this religion in Persia sometime before the sixth century BCE, though new scholarship dates it back to 1200 BCE. Under Cyrus the Great, his teachings became the official state religion of the Persian Empire in the sixth century BCE. Inspired by a vision of the Wise Lord, Ahura Mazda, Zoroaster taught a form of religion that stressed moral choice and personal responsibility. In the cosmic struggle between Good and Evil each individual had to choose between those two opposing forces. Good prevails when human beings follow *Humata* (good thoughts), *Harkta* (good words), and *Huvarshta* (good deeds). The followers of Zoroaster in India are called Parsees. They honor the *Zend-Avesta* as their holy book and represent Ahura Mazda, the omnipresent and invisible God, with fire.

Parsees are few in number, since "true Parsees" are those who are born to two Parsee parents. Parsees have no distinctive dress and few temples. Unlike other religious communities in India, the Parsees leave their dead in "towers of silence" to be eaten by vultures. It is the last and best *Huvarshta*.

Tribal Religions

Eighty-four million Indians are tribal (68 million, according to the 2011 census). In the past two hundred years, 25 to 60 percent of people from among India's tribes have turned to Christianity. The rest practice various forms of animism. Though taking on some aspects of Hinduism, most tribal beliefs fall outside the traditional definition of Hinduism. Believing that numerous gods or spirits live among them and control their world, these animists appease hostile spirits with offerings, animal sacrifices, rituals, and witchcraft.

The Santhals of Orissa and Bengal believe in a hierarchy of spirits who dwell in the sacred groves at the edge of every village. The Bhils, one of the largest tribes of western India, make terracotta horses believed to be spirit riders who accompany the dead on their journey to the afterlife. The traditional religion of the Todas, a small shepherding community in the Nilgiri Hills in South India, is based on buffaloes. Devotees worship at dairy temples. The Nagas of northeast India, once a tribe of headhunters, take great care to pass on genealogies and to appease the dead.

Modern-Day Gods and Gurus
You don't have to look far to find living gods and goddesses in India. Belief in the multiplicity of deities and their *avatars*, and the concept of a guru who leads devotees to truth, make Indian culture the perfect breeding ground for religious sects such as those of Maharishi Mahesh Yogi, Bhagwan Rajneesh, Shree Maa, Satya Sai Baba, and Ammachi, which gained large international followings in the late twentieth century, and continue to do so today.

Hundreds of men and women like these continue to be sought after as miracle workers and revered as incarnations of the divine. Some of them claim to be only gurus, pointing the way for those who follow. Others are worshiped as gods by devotees who enthusiastically call others to find joy, healing, and purpose in their presence.

KARMA AND FATE

Karma may be a distinctly Hindu doctrine, but karmic thinking, or fatalism, affects all Indians, who believe that there is a force outside yourself, a universal or divine power, that controls your life.

Wherever a sinner goes is hell.
Malayalam proverb

In a world where your place is decided by birth and by caste, and major life decisions are made by others, "fate" may be a comfort. "It was his fate" is a common spoken conclusion, whether after a tragic accident to a loved one or a financial windfall to a friend.

Karma is the motivation for a person to do good in order to improve his or her life, if not now, then in the future or the next life; but it can also be a cop-out. *Karma* may be blamed for a bad marriage as well as for bad character, and can be used as an excuse for leaving the poor to their "deserved" fate.

FAMILY

The family is one of the most important and evident of all Indian values. Family in India means the extended family. Whether living under the same roof in the family home or scattered around the globe, family is the entire network of people who are related to each other by blood or marriage.

If everybody tries together even a mountain can be moved.
Malayalam proverb

The extended family maintains and defines social boundaries, ensuring that individuals and single family units stay within the culturally prescribed norms. It is the family that forms identity, where values are passed on and lived out, on whom you depend for life and well-being.

Individuality, autonomy, and independence, highly esteemed values in the West, are antithetical to all that Indians traditionally hold dear. There is no such thing as "my property," "my space," or "my decision." Individuals who act independently are viewed as selfish. Typically those rebels will be corralled through public ridicule or third-party communication (relative A tells relative B who tells relative C until the news comes back to the culprit).

Relationships and social responsibilities are of prime importance, since no one accomplishes anything on their own. Everything, from mothering and naming your children to passing exams, and choosing a spouse, is done with the help of family. It's not uncommon for businesspeople to take time off work to attend the several-day-long wedding of what we might see as a distant relative or to participate in a religious event. These things are viewed as acceptable responsibilities, and people feel obligated, even if not overjoyed, to participate in them. Active participation in life events help to reinforce family identity and belonging, and ensure that just as you are there for others, they will be there for you.

SHAME AND HONOR

When people step outside the boundaries, it is not just the reputation of that individual that is at stake, but the reputation of the family. Honor is an attribute of birth, based on caste and class. Honor can be added to, or diminished, by marriage. But all can be undone by failure to live within the socially prescribed boundaries and cultural values. One bad decision, or one traumatic event beyond your control, and all is lost, never to be regained. This is why the honor (*izzat*) of one's family and community must be upheld at all costs.

> **The reputation lost on a betel nut won't come back though you donate an elephant.**
> *Kannada proverb*

Parents, teachers, relatives, religious and government authorities, and even strangers all know the part they must play in the lives of those around them to hold on to the honor of family, community, and country. Children are taught to align their behavior to communal expectations or face ridicule, or physical punishment. Comparison with the example of others is a common means of teaching what "proper behavior" and expected outcomes are. Mistakes, slipups, and failures, whether moral, behavioral, or academic, are punished and hidden from public view. Honor depends on it.

If honor dies, other things die with it. Families are boycotted; parents have difficulty finding suitable marriage partners for their children; business and social connections may be severed. In extreme cases those who have brought shame to a family or been shamed by their children or spouse may threaten, or commit, suicide.

Gender and Honor

Traditional social attitudes toward women are one of India's cultural paradoxes. The *Laws of Manu*, described on page 20, state that a woman has no existence apart from that of her husband or his family. Yet goddesses are not only worshiped, but are among the most feared of the deities. In the same way, women are placed on a pedestal, revered as pure, and feared as powerful. At the same time they are treated as property—valuable property, but property nonetheless.

Whether pedestal or property, a woman has the power to bring down an entire family. Men are the guardians of family honor, including the honor of their wives, mothers, and sisters. Women, however, bear responsibility not only for their own behavior, but for the behavior of their children and their husband. If any of them are found wanting, she may be blamed for the disgrace that results.

The traditional division of labor in families is one way in which male family members protect their women and so uphold the family honor. This arrangement has payoffs for both parties. A man may take on household responsibilities such as grocery shopping so that his wife or daughters do not have go into the public arena, and are thus protected from abuse, including the all-too-common "eve-teasing" (Indian vernacular for the public sexual harassment of girls and women), thus lessening the likelihood of a tarnished reputation.

In the home, women may add to their honor and that of their family by overseeing household servants. Women of status do not need to clean, cook, or drive—others do it. In the West, machines provide household help, but in India, where nothing is done alone and interdependence meets needs of all kinds within the larger community, a servant means not only prestige for one family, but provision and protection for many people. Though increasing numbers of educated, competent women from all levels of society are working outside the home, cultural pressure to be the traditional wife and mother persists.

The legal rights of women have improved since laws against discrimination were passed in 1993. A milestone on the road to gender equality took place in March 2010 when the Rajya Sabha, the male-dominated upper house of parliament, voted overwhelmingly to reserve a third of all legislative seats across the country for women. Other conditions affecting women show signs of improvement, including the drastic increase in life expectancy for women, from forty-nine years in 1970 to over seventy today.

In spite of new legislation intended to protect women and girls and other healthy progress, violence against women is on the rise—at work, in public, and at home. Wife beating is a common practice, which justified by 47 percent of women and 42 percent of men, according to the 2018 UN Human Development Report.

A foreign woman traveling or living in India will in all likelihood experience the best and the worst of Indian men. Learning a few practical tips (see page 169) can help you avoid unnecessary risks to your person and to your own honor. You would do well to attach yourself to a family, coming under the protection of father and brothers and allowing yourself to be mentored by mother and sisters. It's contrary to many Western values and to some women's sense of self, and it will be frustrating; but it may also be enlightening.

PURITY AND TOLERANCE

Implicit in the concept of honor and shame is the idea of purity. Walking the less than sanitary streets of India, some may find it difficult to believe that purity is a value. But being pure is not about being free of germs. It is about separation from anything or anyone with the power to contaminate honor, morals, caste, or identity.

India is famous for its tolerance. Tolerance has been promoted since the time of Gandhi as an essential part of the process of democratization and secularization, but it is a different kind of tolerance from that promoted in the West. Tolerance is not the acceptance of differences as equally good, right, or valid. It is the acknowledgement that differences must be endured for one's group to survive. In fact, it is not tolerance that is the virtue, but coexistence.

All kinds of people live and work side-by-side in every village and town, but personal distance and social distinctions are maintained by rules and roles that are clear to insiders. For example, family and social taboos on conversion and intermarriage are intended to preserve the purity of the religion and the family bloodline. Indians are proud to note distinctions between their people and all others. Stereotypes help to define boundaries and group identity and values. "We" are like this. "They" are like that. "We" do this. "They" do that. Such simple stereotyping extends to foreigners, too. Movies and TV programs from the West, especially the US, have created an indelible picture of all Westerners as corrupters of morals, religion, and family. Among younger people, the cultural fabric formed by the notions of social and religious purity are visibly fraying as urbanization, education, and globalization challenge traditional Indian mores.

HOSPITALITY, GENEROSITY, AND RECIPROCITY

The warm greeting between friends when they meet; the welcoming smile at the front door; the offer of *chai* when you enter a store—all these are signs of the wonderful hospitality that visitors to India will experience.

Deeply rooted in the idea that the Divine accompanies or dwells in people is the belief that to offer hospitality to a stranger is to serve a god. Indians rarely offer anything but their best to those who enter their homes. Unaware of economic circumstances or social expectations, foreign visitors may not appreciate the extent of the generosity or of all that is sacrificed to provide what, for them, may seem ordinary.

A poor villager may serve an unexpected but important visitor the chicken he had been raising for a special family ceremony. A man returning home after living overseas brings extravagant gifts for his parents, uncles and aunts, extended family members, and a host of family friends. A new friend gives a gold necklace to your newborn baby. Sharing resources, whether through the offering of food to a beggar or the giving of a substantial loan to a friend, serves to sustain individuals as well as to affirm the social order.

This tradition of generosity has been shaped by the patron–client structures of the past. The prosperity of the landowner and the survival of the landless were ensured, as landlords loaned money to clients, who then worked the land to repay the debt. In many cases the debts became so overwhelming that they could never be repaid and generations of bonded laborers served generations of landed gentry. This formula of relationships between social unequals for mutual benefit is still at work today in India's villages, businesses, families, and communities.

While Indians understand what goes on behind the scenes, visitors rarely will. In many cases, the subtext for hospitality or generosity is the expectation of reciprocity. A neighbor looks after your property while you're out of town; you take meals to his ailing grandmother in the hospital. A servant has served your family well for years; you help finance her wedding. While there are few occasions in India where gifts are exchanged, Indians keep a mental balance sheet that enables them to offer appropriate gifts and hospitality to the appropriate people at the appropriate time.

INDIAN STRETCHABLE TIME

IST officially stands for "Indian Standard Time." By now
its conversion to "Indian Stretchable Time" is a well-
worn joke, but not a very funny one for anyone from a
time-oriented culture. Hindi has the same word, *kal*, for
yesterday and tomorrow. Context makes the difference,
and in India it is context, not the clock, that matters. With
some exceptions, Indians are event oriented. They are not
typically late for work, and Indian trains do not wait for
anyone. So it is not the absence of a sense of time, but the
priority of people and events over the clock. For Indians,
time is never "wasted" on people.

To those from places where efficient use of time and visibly
productive work days mean money, respect, and personal
satisfaction, it may be difficult to comprehend the value of
stretchable time. Respect is shown by allowing people to
complete their conversation or business, rather than rushing
on to someone or something else. Bonds are maintained
and new alliances are forged while chatting over tea.

Expect everything to take longer than you think.
One errand that would take thirty minutes back home
may take all morning in India. People may not show up
for appointments, and coworkers may take longer than
agreed upon to finish a project. Give yourself and others
a break by lowering your expectations of what can be
accomplished in a day.

> **There's always a ditch in front of
> someone in a hurry.**
> *Punjabi proverb*

CHAPTER THREE

CUSTOMS & TRADITIONS

HOLIDAYS

India has a great number of holidays, including religious and regional observances, and festivals. Most holiday dates vary annually, based on lunar months or astrologically determined dates.

Bank holidays are typically public holidays, with businesses closed for the day. If you intend to do business while in India, find out in advance about coming dates that mean closed government and other offices. Ask, too, about processions that may block traffic.

Holiday Highlights
Republic Day
All India unites on January 26 for Republic Day, the day it became a sovereign nation. It is a great day to visit New Delhi. Presidential awards are given and a spectacular parade represents every branch of the military, all the states, and the panorama of Indian subcultures.

Independence Day

The celebration of India's independence from the British Empire in 1947 is a huge event across the country. On August 15, schools and businesses close to attend flag-raising ceremonies and to hear the Prime Minister's state of the union address.

Shivaratri

In February, especially in Uttar Pradesh, Hindus may fast during Shivaratri, "the night of Shiva," celebrating his marriage to Parvati.

Holi

Holi, or "burning," is a spring festival. This Hindu celebration of the triumph of good over evil is marked by a bonfire, in which an effigy of the evil Holika is burned, but the meaning of the holiday is overshadowed by the madness of "playing colors." Holi is viewed as a day to ignore social restrictions and taboos. Buckets of colored water and brightly hued paint powders are tossed over neighbor and stranger alike. Nowhere else is Holi celebrated as it is in Varanasi, the center of Shiva worship and famous for its legal *bhang* stores. *Bhang*, ground cannabis leaves mixed with milk and spices, is the official drink of Holi, and often finds its way into edible snacks.

Ramadan

During the month of Ramadan, Muslims over twelve years of age (except pregnant women and the elderly) are expected to abstain from food and drink during daylight hours, and refrain from sinful or selfish behavior. After sunset, family and friends gather to feast, often into early morning. Eid ul-Fitr is the finale of this month-long observance of the revelation of the Koran to Muhammad.

Diwali (Festival of Lights)

Bring earplugs if you plan to sleep during the all-night firecracker-filled festivities that mark the weeklong holiday of Diwali in October. The reasons for celebrating it vary regionally, but the practices of stringing bright lights and giving sweets and gifts are common throughout the country. In the north Indians celebrate Rama's return with his wife, Sita, to Ayodhya after defeating the demon Ravana. Many Hindus light the way for Lakshmi, goddess of wealth, to find her way to their home during this time. Jains celebrate the day their

Small oil lamps are lit for the festival of Diwali, celebrated by Hindus, Sikhs, and Jains.

founder, Mahavira, attained enlightenment. In Bengal, Kali Puja, the worship of the dark goddess, coincides with this festival.

Festivals and Processions
Some festivals are outside the annual calendar. The world's largest is the Kumbh Mela. This "festival of the nectar pot of immortality" is held every three years in one of four locations in North India: Allahabad, Haridwar, Ujjain, and Nasik. In 2013, 100 million devotees converged outside Allahabad for the Maha (great) Kumbh Mela, which occurs every 144 years. By stepping into the place where three rivers—the Ganges, the Yamuna, and the Saraswati (a mythical river)— meet, believers hope to wash away a lifetime of sins.

It seems as though every sacred image, from the elephant-headed Ganesh to the Virgin Mary, is carried through the streets in procession at least once a year. Lifted by devotees or carted through town by ox or, more rarely, elephant, these painted wooden images, festooned with flowers, and sometimes clothes, are taken from the place where they are worshiped to a river for ritual bathing.

Sacred events are relived and retold in art, music, and dance. Mythologies are reenacted in *lilas*, or dramas, by painted children who are paraded through the streets of north India as representations of the gods. Stories are retold in the subtle, graceful movements of classical dancers. Whitewashed street musicians in Tamil Nadu blare horns and beat drums as if in a trance. *Phadas*, folk paintings of western India, honor local heroes

The *rasa lila* dance describes the story of Krishna dancing with Radha and her attendants.

by depicting their stories on cloth. The variety of celebrations and rituals in India is fascinating.

They can, on the other hand, be frustrating for those on business there. Offices may close or be barely functional during major holidays or local festivals; roads may be blocked by processions and crowds; people may be unavailable or preoccupied. There are ways, however, to use these unavoidable events as opportunities—they can be occasions to build personal and cultural bridges. Indians are generally very hospitable. Ask a business acquaintance if you could join their family during a festival. Take them an appropriate gift (see page 97), and don't talk shop. See what normal life is like for them, and ask questions. More trust can be built up on a day like this than in a hundred business meetings.

Processions and *lilas* are not the only reason for suddenly closed businesses or road congestion. You may encounter a political rally. Political temperatures run high, and outsiders cannot always judge when a gathering will turn into an event that requires police intervention. If you are caught on the street when a crowd is incited to riot, or when the police pull out their *lathis* (sticks), go to the nearest shop and ask to stay there until it's all over.

FAMILY EVENTS

Each community in India has its own rites of passage. Most arise from religious beliefs. Some are caste-specific. All are celebrated in ways that highlight the significance not only for the individual, but for the whole community.

Birth

From the moment a baby takes breath, he or she is connected to a family, to a community, to history, and to the Divine through ritual. Life-cycle rituals are as varied as the people who perform them.

A woman typically goes to her maternal home during the last trimester of pregnancy, and remains there until the baby is a month old.

Though the infant mortality rate has drastically reduced in the past fifty years, the historically high rate has shaped traditions surrounding childbirth. In some cases, a child may not be named until he or she is seen to be strong and healthy, being called a pet name or simply "Baby" up till the age of two.

Names are chosen in various ways, depending on the community. Each caste and culture group has its own naming equation. Hindus may consult astrologers for the most auspicious or lucky name. South Indian Christians may choose an anglicized Western or biblical name. In Tamil Nadu boys may be given their own name in addition to the name of their father and grandfather. In Kerala names may include a "house," or clan, indicating one's ancestral family. In any community, you are just as likely to find children named after an Indian movie star as you are a religious hero or deity.

Marriage

Marriage in India can be both holy sacrament and a social or political alliance. The establishment of a new family and the strengthening of the community is so important that parents work hard to find suitable mates for their children, using the extended family, business and

Decorative designs in henna (*mehndi*) are applied to the bride's hands and feet at a ceremony held on the evening before her wedding.

social networks, and their connections to the
Divine, whether astrologer, *imam*, or priest.

Most marriages in India—84 percent—are still
"arranged." To those from individualistic cultures the
practice may seem unfair and even a form of abuse; but
"arranged" does not mean "coerced." It is a system that
has worked for millennia and is irrevocably connected
to India's social system and values. Though, as India's
values change, so do its social customs. Suitability for
marriage is based less on personality and more on
shared caste, class, education, and social standing.

Traditionally, young people live with, and are the
responsibility of, their parents until they marry. Parents
oversee and play a major role in all their life decisions.
Children are strongly dissuaded from pursuing a
profession deemed inappropriate for the family's social
position or for finding a suitable spouse. Good Indian
parents will do whatever they view as necessary to give
their children the best life possible.

Increasingly, young people, especially those living
and working in cities or outside the country, do date and
fall in love. In some instances, this may be kept a secret
because of family expectations and social mores. If the
potential mate is from the right background, the couple
might ask their parents to "arrange" their marriage. But
many Bollywood movies have been made on the premise
of a love story turned to tragedy because of rejection by
the family. And the reality is that fewer than 5 percent
of Indian women are free to choose their husband.

Children of marriageable age and their parents may
use the Internet to increase their pool of potential

matches. The couple has a chance to interact virtually and to be more involved in the decision while maintaining their personal and family virtue.

Religion usually trumps all else in such decisions. To marry outside one's religion is to reject parents, family, and one's very self, and for the same reason conversion to another religion is violently opposed. Both bring loss of honor and opportunity for all concerned.

Though illegal since 1961, dowry remains a fundamental part of Indian marriage. It can be a way for a woman to share in family wealth in a society that, until recently, did not allow women to inherit. But more often the money and gifts do not belong to the girl, but are given to the boy's parents. A girl's family may buy prestige through an alliance with a more educated or wealthy groom. There is also a darker side to this tradition. Dowry deaths, in which the bride becomes the victim of a "kitchen fire," or "suicide," occur nearly every hour in India. Deciding that the dowry was not good enough, the mother-in-law or husband "accidentally" douses her with kerosene and lights a match. But for most Indian couples, dowry is simply one aspect of securing a good lifelong companion.

Child marriage has been illegal in India since 1929, when the British administration determined that twelve was the legal minimum age for marriage. In 1978 this was changed to eighteen for women and twenty-one for men. But for two thousand years Indians from some communities have married off their girl children. Rajputs, the Rajasthani warrior caste, initially gave their young daughters in marriage to prevent their abduction by invaders. Today those who give their children in marriage claim that early marriage protects the girl's purity and prevents unnecessary independence. These days it's predominantly a practice of the poor. Little girls mean little dowry and one less mouth to feed. Because such marriages are not registered with the government, statistics are not definitive. Though marriage of girls under eighteen is declining, 27 percent of girls in India are married before their eighteenth birthday.

Marriage ceremonies and rituals vary according to religion, sect, caste, and region. Because of the importance of marriage and the need to prove prestige, families spend a great amount of money on wedding extravaganzas, often going into debt to do so.

Hindu Weddings

In North India you may see a groom dressed like a king, riding on a white horse. Seated with him may be a small boy—a lucky charm guaranteeing a firstborn son. Surrounded by a hired band, decked out in red uniforms with epaulettes and tasseled fez, the groom's wedding party dances toward the waiting bride.

Though less likely in urban settings, the couple may meet for the first time at the wedding venue as the bride's family greets the groom's, marking their foreheads with red powder. The couple exchanges garlands and makes the first of their vows. With ceremonial gifts and ritualized words, the bride, dressed in a red sari, beautifully bejeweled, and with intricate henna decorations on her hands, is handed over to the groom's family, to whom she now belongs. As the couple walks around the sacred fire, symbolizing their life's journey together, the priest recites

A newly-wed Hindu couple.

sacred *mantras* and further vows are made. During the ceremony, the bride and groom literally "tie the knot." Hands tied together with a string, the pair, now "one," is blessed by their family elders and the priest.

As part of the ceremony, the groom applies a vermilion dot to the bride's forehead. From that day forward, married Hindu women typically wear the red dot or mark (*bindi*). The style of *bindi* varies regionally. Non-Hindus and single women may also wear a *bindi*, but for most it has become purely decorative.

Muslim Weddings

Indian Muslims combine Islamic marriage requirements with Indian tradition. Before the big day, women from both the bride's and the groom's families arrive at her home to participate in festivities that include singing traditional songs and performing rituals that are intended to bring out the bride's beauty. Turmeric paste gives her blushing face a glow, and henna decorations on her hands and feet complement her red sari. A band usually parades before the groom on his way to the ceremony. After the *imam* or *aleem* (priest) delivers a short sermon and recites a few *surahs* (passages) from the Koran, the boy sends a formal proposal to the girl, who must accept for the wedding to take place. Beside mutual consent, there are no specific religious rites for marriage required in Islam. After agreed-upon gifts are exchanged between the families, the marriage contract is signed by the couple, the fathers, and the *imam*.

Islam calls for the groom to give *mehar*—gifts to the bride at the time of the wedding; but in India it is often the practice for a dowry to be given by the girl's family to the boy's. The bride and groom are blessed by their elders and sit down to the wedding feast—though not together. Traditionally, men and women are seated separately. Only after the marriage feast do the bride and groom see each other for the first time. The groom's sister gives the groom the *thaali* (wedding necklace), which he ties around the bride's neck. The *thaali*, or *mangalsutra* (for Hindus), was originally a Hindu ritual that is an important sign throughout India of being a married woman. The bride now becomes part of the groom's family, and tearfully says goodbye to her own. As she enters her new home, her mother-in-law holds the Koran over her head.

Christian Weddings
Many of the same customs are seen in Indian Christian weddings. Engagement ceremonies may occur a week or a day prior to the wedding. Church ceremonies are only a part of the multiday celebration attended by hundreds

or thousands of guests from both families. Wearing white, the bride is escorted up the aisle by her father. Along with the exchange of rings and flower garlands by bride and groom, during the ceremony the girl receives clothing from her new family, which is worn at the reception. There is also the tying of the *thaali*.

Pilgrimage

Pilgrimages are a normal part of life for Indians, and have also become big business. Foreigners from all over the world come to see or participate in them. While Hindu pilgrimage sites predominate, every religion in India has its parallels, and there are thousands of holy sites. Moving away from daily routine to a place full of spiritual meaning and power, pilgrims seek access to, and favor from, their chosen gods.

Varanasi is to Hindus what Mecca is to Muslims. Every day millions of devotees travel there. Many intend to spend their last days there, believing that to die and be cremated inside the city limits is to gain salvation.

A forty-one-day period of penance is part of a pilgrimage to Ayyappa, Kerala, 4,000 feet (1,219m) above sea level in the Western Ghats. Devotees abstain from meat, alcohol, and sex before climbing the mountain, chanting "*Samiye Saranam Ayyappa*" ("O, Lord Ayyappa, I come to thee for refuge"). Woman of childbearing age or men with recently cut hair or shaven faces are forbidden to enter the temple. In special backpacks, pilgrims carry articles for doing *puja* to Ayyappa, specific food to enable them to make the long trek, and a small blanket.

A BLESSING FROM THE GODS

No Hindu celebration is complete without *prasad*—food that has been offered to a deity. If you are offered *prasad*, typically a sweet, it is proper to take it with your right hand and immediately put it into your mouth. It is believed to be infused with the power or blessing of the god to whom it was offered. Indians of other faiths will probably not be offered it out of respect for their religion. You don't need to eat it if it is contrary to your own convictions. Refusing *prasad*, if done with humility and respect for those offering it, will not offend anyone. You will be respected for holding to your own form of devotion.

For nine days in September, tens of thousands of pilgrims move toward Tirupati, Andhra Pradesh, to the shrine of Sri Venkateswara, Lord of Seven Hills. Standing for hours, pilgrims line up just to catch a glimpse of the deity and to rub camphor, or present recently shorn hair as an offering. Daily rituals, which include waking the god and putting him to sleep, can be made in the name of a devotee—for a price. The temple of Tirupati Tirumala Balaji is one of the wealthiest religious sites in the world, second only to the Vatican.

The "Lourdes of the East" is found in Velankanni, in Tamil Nadu. During a ten-day festival in

September, Catholics and many others come to this most popular of all Indian shrines looking for miracles. Since the sixteenth century people have reported appearances of Our Lady of Velankanni asking for milk for her baby boy, curing the lame, and requesting a chapel to be built in her name. Because of the hundreds of healings that have taken place there, this manifestation of the Virgin is called *Arokia Matha*, or Mother of Good Health.

Death

With 27,000 people dying daily in India, rituals surrounding death are a common sight.

Hindu Rituals

Bathed, clothed, and covered with flowers, a body is carried to the cremation grounds. While infants and small children may be buried or enshrouded and set adrift on a holy river, Hindus typically cremate their dead.

Women grieve at home. Only male relatives and friends gather around the funeral pyre, while priests perform the last rites and the eldest son lights the fire that will release the spirit of the deceased to be reborn. When the body is burned and the proper rituals are complete, the bone fragments and ashes are scattered on a river.

The family remains ritually "polluted" for a number of days, unable to perform *puja* at the family shrine, participate in religious events, or visit the homes of others. Pictures of the deceased are displayed in the home and adorned with garlands, and small plates of food are offered to the spirit of the loved one. Memorials take place during the first week, on the thirty-first day, and on the first anniversary. It is disrespectful for anyone to marry during the year after the death of an immediate family member.

Widows, traditionally dressed in white, could not remarry. In the past, and even in some remote areas today, a Hindu widow, tied to her husband in this life and the next, would throw herself on to his funeral pyre.

Muslim Rituals

Muslims believe in prompt burial following a ritual cleansing of the body. Muslim women are not allowed at funerals. Male relatives lift the bier, carrying the carefully wrapped body to the burial ground. The deceased is placed in the ground facing toward the Ka'bah in Mecca, ready for resurrection on the Day of Judgment. Male mourners throw earth into the grave

Muslim funeral procession.

as they recite a verse from the Koran. Tombstones should not be near the grave. Feasts of remembrance are held on the fortieth day, at four, six, and nine months, and on the first anniversary.

Christian Rituals

Family comes from near and far to mourn, or to comfort those who mourn, the loss of a loved one. The body is carried to the church cemetery in a coffin, or sometimes on a palanquin, accompanied by family and community, and a priest or pastor who performs a traditional Christian funeral. The family will visit the cemetery on Christian holidays and other important occasions. They mark death anniversaries and refrain from arranging marriages during the one-year mourning period.

SUPERSTITIONS AND OMENS

India, full of people of faith, is also filled with a vast store of what outsiders might consider superstitions and belief in omens that shape daily life and foretell future events. While many of these arise from religious stories, most are commonly held across religious, caste, and subcultural lines. Many beliefs and practices are related to the fear of being cursed.

Some Traditional Superstitions

- To see a crow fly over your house is a bad omen. A crow cawing signals the arrival of guests.

Seeing a peacock is lucky. Hearing a peacock is unlucky. An owl is a warning to prepare for tragedy.

- A dream of marriage is lucky. A dream of death is unlucky. Dreams have meanings, and should be paid attention to, especially if you dream of a departed ancestor coming to you with a message.

- Itching eyes may indicate that someone is jealous of you and is planning your demise. Jealousy is a constant worry in India and special precautions are taken to protect oneself from this dangerous destroyer. Amulets and charms worn on a wrist, the hand of Fatima painted on a wall, or fasting prayer are believed to ward off the "evil eye."

- Days of the week and specific dates matter when planning marriages, long-distance travel, or new construction. Hindus will consult an astrologer before making any important plans.

- At home, the direction you lay your head in bed can determine your future happiness. *Tulsi* (basil) trees outside your door bring good fortune.

- A bride must step into her husband's home for the first time with her right foot, or misfortune will strike.

- If you are invited to a wedding, be sure not to give knives (which "cut" relationships) or cut flowers (dead items, fit for the dead). Cash is always safe, but must be given in odd numbers. You will surprise the couple by giving it in the culturally appropriate way: single bills.

CLOTHES MAKE THE MAN (AND WOMAN)

Most men in India wear Western-style shirts and trousers. During the time of the Independence Movement, Gandhi made *kadhi*, handwoven cotton, popular. Today the *kadhi kurta* (Indian-style shirt) is still the choice for politicians. It is often worn with a *dhoti*, a white rectangular cloth wrapped to form loose pants. The *dhoti* used to be worn daily, and still is in many villages, but over most of India today it is worn only for special occasions. In the south, *lungis*, patterned cotton sarongs, may be worn by men at home and by some workers in public.

Elegant and colorful saris and practical *shalwar kameez*—long trousers and a long tunic top—are still typical dress for women. Other women's wear varies regionally and is often based on age or life stage. Young women today often wear jeans with an Indian-style top.

Though you can't tell it from Hindi films, modesty is important. Women should not show too much skin, even when wearing a sari. The *dupatta* (scarf) and the *pallu* (end of the sari) are traditionally used to cover head, shoulders, breasts, and midriff from male view. Even modestly dressed women may be accused of using their eyes to seduce men. To avoid miscommunicating when in public, women should not look men in the eye, or intentionally touch a man. Humility and even invisibility entitle a woman to the "good" label in Indian society.

CHAPTER FOUR

MAKING FRIENDS

FRIENDSHIP

Friendship for Indians does not mean a casual acquaintance, but a lifelong attachment. Childhood friends, school classmates, and college roommates provide companionship, a sense of place, and relational and vocational opportunity throughout one's lifetime.

Indians tend to be affectionate and expressive, with a deep sense of loyalty and belonging. People go out of their way to meet their friends' needs and to be present and actively helpful during trouble. Many are even willing to risk life and livelihood for one another. If an Indian considers you a friend, you have entered into a relationship—and a network of relationships—that will bring joy and also responsibility, for friendship brings with it expectations that are not always anticipated by Westerners.

In individualistic or work-focused societies, we may call a friend after several weeks, or even months, and expect to pick up where we left off. In India, prolonged silence or absence of spontaneous visits can result in hurt feelings and damaged relationships: friends are "family," and require a higher degree of commitment.

Foreigners and Friendship

It's not difficult to strike up an acquaintance in India. Indians are curious about foreign visitors and more than willing to enter into conversation. Shopkeepers offer *chai* (tea) or a "cold drink" as you step in from the heat. People on the street offer help when you look lost. Fellow train passengers will gladly share their food (warning you with a smile that "it might be too spicy for you"). Students and others will want to practice their English. The extensive use of English initially makes finding friends easier.

Indian body language, social cues, and assumptions differ so greatly from those in the West that it may be difficult for someone just entering the country to discern who has the potential for becoming a true friend, and who is befriending you merely for personal gain. This is a constant source of tension for Americans and Europeans, who may be seen as having the power to help people into affluence and opportunity, whether through networks, gifts of cash, or even marriage. It's especially tricky as true friends are expected to share resources and offer assistance and support, financially and socially, as well as emotionally. A not-so-subtle indication of a financial need or a direct request for a business connection is perfectly acceptable among friends. So how do you know who your friends are? You will discover them when you are in need. Your Indian friends will be there for you in ways that may surprise and humble you.

MAKING CONVERSATION

Getting Started

Greetings in India are a matter of both showing and receiving respect. But how can you respectfully greet people in a country with twenty-two official languages and a seemingly infinite number of subcultures? Don't worry. It's probably apparent at first glance that you are a visitor, and no one will expect you to know all their ways. Surprise them. Learn a few helpful phrases (see page 189) and observe how Indians of your age and gender greet others.

Whether in English or with your newly acquired local phrases, introduce yourself to people in the neighborhood. Ask to accompany your host or a new friend to the market or on an errand, or invite them to go with you somewhere. Drop in on a colleague, saying you'd like their help to understand your new surroundings.

Topics of Conversation

Everywhere you go in India, people will ask you the same questions: What's your name? Where are you from? What are you doing? When are you going home? (For those staying longer-term, the last question may feel offensive. But don't take it personally. It probably comes from the perspective that one's primary place is with one's family and community.) Have ready a brief description of yourself and your family, especially if you are living in India. You may want to cover the essentials without giving away information you, or they, feel is inappropriate. For example, many Indians are not shy to ask about money issues, including your income. If such topics embarrass you, be prepared with an ambiguous answer.

Many topics viewed as personal are fair game in India. Indians do not hesitate to talk politics. They will ask your opinion of your own country's policies (of which they are well aware), as well as of India's politics and world issues. They will comment on child-rearing practices, attire (especially if a foreign woman is wearing a sari or *shalwar kameez*), and appearance. They will freely share information about their children's academic successes, and will want to hear about your own children's education and aptitudes. If you are single and over twenty-five, they will ask you why you're not married, and will advise you on finding a suitable spouse. If you are a woman planning to live in India for any length of time, prepare for questions about your whole family and why you've abandoned them. Although many Indian men live abroad for educational or financial reasons, it's less common for single or unaccompanied Indian women. Your reasons may not make sense to your new friends. Don't expend too much energy trying to help people understand you. They can't. But they can still learn to love and trust you over time.

Taboos

Indians generally do not discuss sexual matters, including dating, boyfriends or girlfriends, marital or family problems, or children's misbehavior or poor academic performance. If an Indian asks questions on these topics or offers unsolicited information about his or her sex life or marriage problems, you can be sure that this is not culturally acceptable. It is time to end the conversation. Because of the diversity of beliefs in India, religion may be avoided as a topic of conversation in a social setting.

Yes and No

Like much of Indian culture, the use of "yes" and "no" may confuse and confound visitors. But Indians understand exactly what is being said.

"Yes" is a cord that ties people together. Indians will say "yes" to maintain a relationship and their honor. It's shameful to refuse a request or to be ignorant of a helpful answer. In general, Indians will drop whatever they are doing to meet the needs of family, community, or guest, and whether you're asking if they know the way to the station or if they can take you there, you will usually hear a "yes." Make sure, if the information or instruction is important, to ask more than one person. Indians do it all the time. They know what "yes" means.

One important phrase you need to know is: "I will try." If you invite someone to an event or a party, or have asked for some specific help, and they respond, "I will try," they have just declined. They value your friendship, and don't want to risk offending you with a straight refusal. So expect them to be absent or unavailable.

"No" will be the answer to your offer to help or serve them. The key is to ask three times. If, after the third offer, your friend still says "no," it's a true no. You will be considered polite if you do the same. For instance, when offered food the first time, politely decline. In all likelihood you will be asked again. If so, simply say "yes, thank you." If not, it means they're used to Westerners.

Next time with that friend you'll know to say "yes" the first time.

Personal Space
You may find a great disparity between your sense of personal space and the close proximity of both friend and stranger. If you don't look Indian, be prepared to be stared at everywhere outside the major cities. Curious folk may summon up the courage to touch the hair of a fair-haired girl.

There is a lot of hand-holding in India, but not across gender. Men may hold hands as they walk down the street. Boys of all ages drape their arms around each other. Girls and women often greet one another with a kiss on the cheek, and clasp hands as they share stories. These are all signs of affection and friendship, and should not be mistaken for sexual behavior.

As a visitor to India it is never appropriate to hold hands with, or express affection, physically or verbally, to someone of the opposite sex. Handshaking is a common and usually acceptable greeting when you're in a city, but not always. If you are introduced to a woman, wait for her to extend her hand first. (For more details, see page 188.)

GIVING

Who Pays?
In India, whether you invite someone for a cup of coffee or an expensive banquet, you are expected to pay the

bill. Don't expect others to pay their share. They won't. If a friend invites you, you can expect him or her to insist on paying. Feel free to argue, or make sure that you extend the invitation next time.

Gift Giving

Everyone loves gifts, but in India they are an important aspect of establishing and maintaining relationships. Twenty-four-carat gold jewelry, electronics, and other expensive gifts are given by family and close friends to newborns and newlyweds, and on special occasions.

Because of the need to maintain equilibrium in relationships through reciprocity, expensive gifts from a visiting friend or business partner may produce a sense of obligation and stress that will create a barrier to the relationship in the future. As a visitor or foreign guest, you should not feel compelled to compete with gifts given by Indians to Indians.

If you receive an expensive gift, or hospitality is lavished on you in a way that feels excessive, do not feel obliged to return in kind. Keep gifts simple and meaningful. A box of sweets, a basket of fruit, or a specialty from your own country is a thoughtful gift when visiting a friend for the first time. If you bring chocolate from home, make sure you carry it in your hand luggage and give it to people you meet at the beginning of your journey. Chocolate sold in India has a higher wax content to keep it stable in high temperatures.

Small toys or an English book will make children smile. Anything that shows where you come from—a calendar with photos, for example—will be valued by your new friends. Other welcome gifts might be brand-name cosmetics and perfumes, moderately priced pens, or T-shirts from a local university or sports team. If you are on a smaller budget, candy bars, hot chocolate packets, barrettes, or postcards from home are perfectly acceptable.

Most Indians, whether Hindu, Muslim, or Christian do not drink alcohol, so make sure that it is acceptable before giving wine or spirits. Leather may not be appropriate either, for religious reasons. A man should not give jewelry or flowers to a woman, as it is considered too personal; and, as we've seen, cut flowers are not generally valued as a gift, specially not for a wedding.

If you didn't bring gifts from home you'll need help to find culturally appropriate local gifts. The things you find beautiful in India are not always prized by Indians. A basket of fruit is appreciated when visiting a home, and cash inside a greeting card is good for special occasions. Better still, ask friends and acquaintances for suggestions, though be prepared to hear, "No need." Disregard that advice and take a gift.

When Giving Is Not Friendship

Beggars will greet you everywhere. If you are in India to stay, you will have time to understand the system and to make decisions regarding how to respond to them and the soul-piercing poverty visible at every turn. Don't be duped by the wide eyes of a child, the bandaged hands of a leper, or your own emotions. If you give them money it will go to others, may not benefit them at all, and will help to perpetuate the cycle of poverty, into which these people were born. If you would like to help the 1.5 million who have been reduced to begging by profession, disease, or enslavement, there are many excellent agencies, Indian and otherwise, that could use your money to do lasting good.

VISITING AN INDIAN HOME

Hospitality

People you've just met may invite you home for tea, dinner, or even for a short stay. To show appreciation for their hospitality, take a small gift, such as a box of sweets. You will be warmly greeted at the door and shown where to put your shoes, which should be taken off before entering. Slippers are not typically provided. Shoes are considered unclean, so no good host would offer a guest footwear worn by others.

There is a proper protocol to an evening in an Indian home. No matter what time you enter a home, with or without an invitation, you will immediately be offered *chai* (tea with milk, sugar, and sometimes spices), coffee (with milk and sugar), water, juice, or sherbet (a popular fruit- or flower-flavored drink.) It is impolite to refuse.

In India, people converse first, eat later. Once the meal is over, everyone knows it's time to go home. People may sit and chat for hours while a foreign guest, possibly used to eating first and conversing after the meal, or having extended conversations over a multicourse meal, may wonder why dinner is not being served. Dinner can happen at any time in the evening. Even families with small children will eat late.

Indians in cities and towns eat at a table. In villages, in a poorer home, or at an event with many guests, people may be seated on mats. The women of the house will have spent all day preparing food for an invited guest. Guests may be served the meal alone or with the head of the household. This is a sign of honor. In homes where food may be scarce, it also ensures that guests eat as much as they want without the family being shamed by running out of food. Dessert is not always served at the end of a meal. You will know it's over when the family members get up to wash their hands. Then it's time to thank the hosts for a wonderful meal, say goodbye to everyone present, and leave. You won't be left until you are outside the gate, down the street, or in a car or taxi. It's a sign of connection and protection that is an integral part of all Indian relationships.

Table Manners

You will be offered aromatic foods with copious amounts of rice or perfectly round handmade *chapattis* until you either leave a small amount of food on your plate or refuse by putting your right hand over your plate. When offered the first time, it's polite to decline. You will be asked again.

Indian food tastes better when eaten with one's fingers. Use your right hand.

There is always provision for washing your hands before and after a meal. Many Indian dining rooms are fitted with a basin for this purpose. Generally, food should touch only your fingertips, up to the first knuckle. Though people will be polite if you dirty your whole fingers or the palm of your hand, they will be disgusted. If you feel too uncomfortable or make too much of a mess eating with your fingers, feel free to ask for a spoon.

During a meal, it's acceptable to use your left hand to serve yourself or others, but you probably won't have to. The women of the household will be standing at the ready to serve. In fact, it is not polite to reach for food, and you should never have to ask. It will be offered. If it's not offered, it may be an indication that demand exceeds supply. So take your cue from your Indian hosts. You can tear *chapattis*, *nan*, or *parathas* using two hands. Outside close family, it is never polite to touch someone else's food or eat off another's plate, and never drink from someone else's glass.

Observing these few points of etiquette will make your visit more enjoyable for you and your hosts. But regardless of your manners or mistakes, you can be sure that all your needs will be met with the greatest possible care and generosity. Besides food and drink, you may well be offered a place to stay, connections in other parts of India, and a ride or an escort to your next destination. It's a matter of friendship for your host to extend every resource for your benefit. They are bound to treat you, their guest, as they've been taught to do in every Indian home and all of India's legends—as a god.

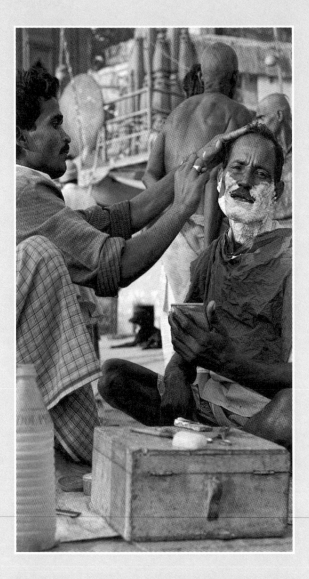

CHAPTER FIVE

PRIVATE & FAMILY LIFE

NOT SO PRIVATE

Looking Without Seeing

You may find the word "private" in Indian language dictionaries. You will not, however, find much privacy in India—or not in ways you recognize. Westerners define privacy in terms of personal space, confidential information, and freedom from intrusion. But in India, in general, privacy is not about what's hidden, but about what's ignored.

Indians develop the skill of looking without seeing early on. In many rural areas, fields double as toilets. In towns, teenage boys in *lungis* or shorts can be found soaping up at the public water pump. In the river, women discreetly wash and change. Large numbers of people share small spaces: an extended family lives in a tiny two-room hut; a couple and their children share a bedroom in an urban apartment. In spite of obvious deterrents to intimacy, eighteen million babies are born in India each year.

Looking without seeing is difficult for a visitor who is bombarded by new sights; but out of respect for the privacy of those around you, learn to ignore them.

In an Indian family home there's no such thing as personal space. You may drop in on a friend to find them and their family, or friends, comfortably gathered on a bed for a chat or a nap. Bedrooms are considered common space, and people don't usually knock before entering. Even hotel staff may give only a cursory rap on the door as they open it. If privacy matters to you, you will need to lock doors. Saying "Please wait here. I'll be right back" may work, but only some will take the hint.

Bathrooms are the exception. You will get some privacy there, though on a rare occasion even a woman will find a public toilet has no stall door.

Possessions, too, are not "mine," but "ours." Family and close friends may borrow all kinds of things from one another, including money, often without seeing the necessity of returning it. It's not theft or thoughtlessness. It's communal property.

Photo Op?

If you were at the other end of your camera, would you want your picture taken in that situation? If not, think twice before you take the photograph.

Family Secrets

Indians do keep some things private, hidden even from close friends and extended family. Mental illness, depression, and sexual and physical abuse are discussed fairly openly in many Western societies. In India such things are intensely guarded secrets that must not be exposed. Family reputation, social status, and the marriageability of daughters are at stake.

You may feel no qualms about relaying your family's mental health history, personal or even general stories of abuse or divorce, but Indian taboos on these topics will ensure that if you choose to share those "private" matters, respect and trust will be lost. Your friends may suddenly seem to be uncomfortable around you.

THE FAMILY HOME

Contrasts and Conveniences

Flying into any major airport in India, you will get a glimpse of the many kinds of places people call "home." Delhi's and Kolkata's high-rise blocks; Mumbai's and Chennai's masses of shingle-roofed lean-tos; Kerala's whitewashed houses surrounded by lush tropical gardens; the blue and pink rooftop terraces of Rajasthan.

On the train you will pass some of India's six hundred thousand villages. Thatched roofs atop bright blue plastered dwellings, small clusters of homes with red-tiled roofs, and wooden huts on stilts above green paddy fields house the 66 percent of India's rural population.

In every town and city you're confronted with the uncomfortable juxtaposition of rich and poor. Slums visible from the villas of the wealthy; day laborers from city outskirts sleeping on sidewalks outside the apartment complexes they're building to shelter middle-class families; homeless families doing the best they can with a piece of plastic and a few scrounged bits of metal or wood.

Though "home" can be a single room in a multifamily dwelling or a multistoried marble mansion, for most, the family home is not very different from one in any other part of the world: a place to sleep, sit, and cook. Wooden or woven platforms called *chaarpaai* provide seating for many people, but middle-class homes have living rooms complete with couches, chairs, and, in the cities, TVs. Bedrooms are typically shared. It's not uncommon for a mother and her children to sleep together in the same bed. Kitchens are functional spaces filled with steel or brass pots. Sometimes there is an outside kitchen, where the women or servants prepare the more labor-intensive dishes or foods that might create unpleasant odors indoors. You may find a refrigerator in the dining room, along with a porcelain basin for washing hands before and after meals. Many Indian homes have a space set apart for worship or prayer. Hindus may have a small shrine where women perform daily rituals for the well-being of their families.

Middle-class homes have bathrooms and toilets. If there's no shower, there will be a bucket and a cup; guests are generally expected to bring their own toiletries and towels. The toilet may be separate. Indians do not generally use toilet paper; instead you will find water and a cup. If you do find paper, it's usually disposed of in a waste receptacle, rather than flushed after use.

A Day in the Life

Most women in India are up before sunrise to get ready for the day. Usually with the help of servants or other women in the home, they prepare breakfast and perform the necessary daily religious rituals before waking the men and children. After breakfast everyone gets to their work, whether outside or inside the home.

The laundry man or woman comes by the house each week to deliver cleaned and pressed laundry, and to collect more washing. An ironing trolley may be found at the end of the block for pressing needs. All manner of household goods can be bought right outside the home, from milk and eggs to brooms and buckets.

Meal preparation is typically a full-time occupation for many women. For those without the luxury of refrigeration, groceries must be purchased daily. The

Groceries, household items, and snacks are readily available on the streets.

butcher or the fishmonger knows his customers and what they usually buy. Stopping by the vegetable stall, an Indian woman orders what she needs, knowing the vendor's son will deliver it in time to prepare the evening meal. Though most people continue to shop in local markets or family-owned stores, in the last decade, supermarkets have sprung up in urban India, filled with frozen and quick-fix foods, changing meal preparation time and the family dinner table.

People eat two to four times a day, depending on income, occupation, and lifestyle. Lunch is the main meal. Public schools may provide children with a lunch of rice and *dhal* (lentils). Most schoolchildren, and their working parents, carry a *tiffin* (steel lunchbox, or stacked set of boxes) holding freshly cooked food from home. "Tea" in the early evening can be anything from *chai* (tea) to *tiffin* (in this case, a light supper or hearty snack).

Teatime is visiting time. Friends, business colleagues, or family from across town will drop in to chat. Families sit down to their evening meal between 8:00 and 11:00 p.m.

Extended family expectations and needs, children's school and tutoring, two working parents, frequent guests and drop-in visitors, traffic and transportation chaos, and long commutes in the city all contribute to the stress of daily life. But in this interdependent society, networks of mutually beneficial relationships ease the strain.

Most women do not have to manage household responsibilities alone. Extended family nearby, or even in the same house, means that mothers-in-law, sisters, aunts, and cousins help with food preparation, child care, and other aspects of daily home management.

Traditional caste and class divisions of labor and continued low levels of education, especially for women, contribute to the widespread practice of keeping servants. Both day and live-in servants help with chores in the home, drive children to school, run errands, and serve as security guards at night. Wages are low, but include food and, for resident servants, a roof over their heads. Abuse of all kinds does, of course, happen. But for many these arrangements provide sustenance and practical help as well as accessibility to the service and resources of an even larger network.

Family Structures

As this is a traditional culture, the husband and father is considered the head of the Indian home. When multiple generations live in the same house, the eldest male is king. The wife and mother, however, also has a powerful place in the hierarchy.

The primary relationship is between the mother and her firstborn son. Her place in the family is elevated by the birth of a son who becomes, in effect, her retirement plan. The eldest son traditionally bears the responsibility to care for his parents, financially and physically, in their old age. Who he marries matters not only for him, but also for his parents and unmarried sisters.

India still boasts the lowest divorce rate on the planet—only 1 percent. But three times that many couples choose separation. And there are indicators of a drastic culture shift taking place affecting Indian family life. Isolation from extended family, financial independence for women, career and time pressures for double-income couples, greater education and understanding of legal rights, and media-spawned changes in marital expectations are redefining not only marriage but also identity among younger generations.

Women's Work

The strength of Indian women is seen in every family, whether she is a wife caring for home and family, a corporate CEO managing hundreds of employees, or a laundress beating clothes by the river. Since the opening up of the Indian economy in the 1990s, the number of women working in government and the private sector has doubled. Women are becoming financial contributors to family wealth and status. The increase in education and vocational opportunity may slowly change how women are viewed in families and in society.

Women comprise a mere 15 percent of the formal workforce. It is estimated that nearly 90 percent of all working women in India are not counted among "working women." They labor in fields, in construction, and as domestic servants for little or no pay. Considered physically and intellectually weaker than men, women in employment are paid less than their male counterparts, and their work at home is taken for granted. Even when a young woman receives a good education and income, these are still viewed as assets for the marriage market. Starting a business, developing a career, or taking on upper-level management responsibilities remains difficult for women who, in general, are still held fully responsible for running the home and family. Tragically, as the number of women in the marketplace has climbed, so has violence against women. Rape, kidnap, torture, and beatings have all risen sharply in the past decade.

CHILDREN

Bringing Up Baby

Though every family is different, Indian parents have common values. They willingly make sacrifices for the good of their children, even if it means the father has to work in a distant city or country to earn enough for a proper education or the mother goes without adequate food to see her children well nourished.

A close bond is created between mother and child by constant physical contact throughout infancy and childhood. Children share the mother's bed, may receive a daily oil massage, and may be breastfed until two or

three years of age. When old enough to eat solid food, the child is fed from the mother's hand. Even when children are older, mothers make sure that on special occasions, such as a birthday, special foods come from her hand.

Sweets are often used to keep babies and children from fussing. Many common practices used to keep babies happy appear overindulgent to Western eyes. But these actions not only stop tears and tantrums, they develop a deep sense of interdependence, in contrast to Western parenting, which has traditionally been geared to develop independence and autonomy.

Indian children are never alone, even when they sleep, and the common Western practice of teaching an infant to sleep in a separate room may be seen as abuse by good Indian parents. Infants and toddlers are carried throughout the day by mother, aunts, older siblings, or servants. Children of all ages are expected to play together and to look after each other. It's from older siblings, cousins, and neighbors that younger children learn the rules of social order and the respect for hierarchy.

Boys learn early that they have a special place in the order of things. Mothers jealously guard their relationship with their sons, not only while they are children but into adulthood. While girls learn how to take care of home and family, boys are given little responsibility, except for doing well in school. Boys are spiritually safeguarded, as well: in some parts of India male infants may be dressed as girls or have a black dot drawn on their cheek with kohl to ward off jealousy and the evil eye.

Whether male or female, middle class or villager, social expectations shape and supersede personal aspirations and desires as children grow into adulthood. Despite this, there is a deep strain of romance evident among teenagers and single young adults. Crushes on the opposite sex, tinged with Bollywood-style fantasies about love, are prevalent.

Boys and girls (as they are called through college) may be segregated in school and social settings as they grow older to prevent inappropriate emotional entanglements or sexual misconduct. Romantic love is equated with sexual activity. Because the majority of marriages in India are still arranged, even the suspicion of improper conduct can bring tragedy or ruin, especially for the girl, for the sisters of both parties, and for the reputation of the extended families. Parents help teenagers, by any means necessary, to focus their energies on education, to work for the benefit of the family, and to uphold the respect of the family name.

Education

Today 1.3 million primary and secondary schools, 41,500 colleges and universities, and innumerable private institutions offer education to the next generation. India's children have a constitutional right to free education to the age of fourteen, which is compulsory. For decades the government has instituted programs to promote education for all. More children are in school than ever before in India's history — 98 percent. And more are graduating from secondary school than previous generations. Female literacy rates have risen dramatically and more girls are registering for, and remaining in, school. In an effort to give greater

Chemistry class in a secondary school in Delhi.

opportunity for social uplift to underprivileged communities, the law requires a certain number of places in tertiary institutions to be reserved for "scheduled castes and tribes." Still, the average dropout rate is 10 percent overall and 60 percent for girls. And only 10 percent have access to higher education.

Middle- and upper-class families can afford the best available private education. This is becoming popular due to its increasing affordability, even for poorer families. Forty percent of Indian's children are enrolled in private schools—a radical shift from even a decade ago. But because private schools do not have to be recognized by the government, quality varies. In rural areas, low teaching standards, high teacher absenteeism, sparse funding, lack of public services such as electricity and water, traditional gender bias, family poverty, and child malnutrition contribute to the 40 percent rural student dropout rate.

For those children who remain in school, there is enormous pressure to be top of the class. Competition is a stressful component of childhood in India. Formal education and the pressure to be "first rank" begins at the age of three. In nursery and kindergarten, children learn to read and write in their mother tongue and in Hindi, or English. By the end of secondary school, at age seventeen or eighteen, students' vocational and educational options have been determined by their exam results. The cream of the crop may choose to attend one of India's top higher education institutions, such as an IIT (Indian Institute of Technology), or to become an international student in the US, the UK, Australia, Germany, or Canada.

If aptitude or exam results are not enough to qualify one's child for the desired Indian institution, "donations" or personal gifts can open the door. Corruption is a sad fact of educational life in India. Cheating in exams and papers are often viewed as a "right" rather than a wrong. Concerned families may pay tens of thousands of rupees to change the outcome of their son's or daughter's poor university entrance exam.

THE HOLY AND THE UNHOLY

There are groups of people living outside traditional family structures. Some are revered, others disdained, but all are kept at a distance and each one plays a valuable role in the very society that requires them to remain outside.

Sadhus

In a quest for personal enlightenment, millions of Indian men and women live as Hindu ascetics, or *sadhus*. Casting off family and communal responsibilities as well as worldly possessions and comforts, these voluntary outcastes can be seen in every corner of India. Considered "holy" by Hindus, *sadhus* are part of the Indian landscape.

Many *sadhus* are known for their spiritual teaching and are sought for blessing. A few evoke dread due to their occult powers and grotesque practices. Some wander alone, having taken a vow of silence. Others become part of a community devoted to a particular god, their divine allegiances identified by the color and pattern of forehead markings. It's common to see saffron-robed men sit along the street, wooden bowl in hand, begging for food or coins. During a festival you may see *Nagababas* ("naked fathers") parading en masse, with ash-covered bodies and long, matted hair. Revered by some as gods, feared because of their power to bless and to curse, *sadhus* are a visible reminder to Hindus of the unreality of the material world.

Hijras and the "Third Gender"

Only in India is it possible to be simultaneously holy and unholy. *Hijras* embody this unique Indian perspective. According to the first official count in 2014, there are half a million eunuchs (by birth, by force, or by choice) who are now legally India's "third gender." Identifying themselves as neither male nor female, they are not homosexual, nor do they fit

India's transgender community (*hijras*) stretches back to antiquity and is mentioned in ancient texts such as the *Mahabharata* and the *Kama Sutra*.

contemporary definitions of transgender. Though unable to legally marry, *hijra* communities "marry" within their community and form "families" of "sisters." They follow a hierarchy that includes gurus, and can be punished and cast out for not following the rules of their community.

Using coarse language to embarrass, or making sexual advances to intimidate, *Hijras* solicit money from the public. Some show up uninvited, but not unexpectedly, at weddings. Payment leads to blessing newlyweds with fertility. Refusal results in verbal abuse and curses. When they sing and dance outside the home of a newborn boy, parents must pay them to avoid their child being cursed.

CHAPTER SIX

TIME OUT

In India "leisure" depends very much on where one lives, one's status, family expectations, work demands, discretionary income, and accessibility to ideas and options. For village India, "leisure" is built into daily life and varies with the seasons. It varies even among the 31 percent of the population who live and work in towns and cities. Many work a six-day week. Some reserve a specific weekday for religious observances. For most, Saturday and Sunday are "the weekend."

On weekends, movie theaters are packed with groups of teenage friends and families. Indian families take short excursions by car or bus to nearby cities, visiting family or watching festival activities. They may visit a temple, take in a movie, and have a meal in a restaurant. For women who are responsible for a home and family, their "leisure" time may be consumed with meal preparation for family outings, housework, and other activities related to entertaining visitors. Clubbing is common for the young middle classes in large metropolitan cities like Delhi, Mumbai, and Chennai.

Many families get away for extended holidays during the hot summer months. In the past few years, vacationing abroad has become possible for India's middle class, or the affordable railways take people to popular destinations inside the country. The beaches of Goa, the backwaters of Kerala, and the "hill stations" of Ooty, Kodaikanal, and Shimla remain popular destinations for vacationing families. But 97 percent of Indians tend to travel primarily for spiritual reasons, visiting the sacred sites found around every corner of this country.

EATING OUT

Everywhere you turn you'll find restaurants and *dhabbahs* (rustic outdoor cafés) serving regional, national, and international foods. American fast-food outlets, such as KFC, Subway, and McDonald's, are popular in the cities, offering country-specific menu items you won't find in the US or Europe. For example, burgers in India may be lamb, not beef, and there are always vegetarian options.

Restaurants have varying degrees of hygiene in the dining rooms and the kitchens. The cleanliness of the public eating area is probably a good indication of the standard in the kitchen.

Street Vendors

Ten million street vendors all over India sell food, and you need never go hungry if you have a few rupees. In the south, huge *dosai* (rice pancakes) fried in *ghee*

TIPPING

Tipping is common practice in restaurants and hotels. In upscale eating establishments you may be charged a 15 to 20 percent "luxury tax," which is a mandatory tip, and there's no need to add more. In other restaurants, just leave a few rupees rather than a percentage.

- Hotel porters may be tipped 5 to 10 rupees per bag, or when providing exceptional service.
- In most cases, cab drivers and *dhabbah* waiters do not require a tip.
- Household servants, drivers, and those who regularly serve you can be given gifts of money on special occasions. In those situations it's understood as *baksheesh*—a gift made in advance in order to get the job done.

(clarified butter) until crisp and filled with savory potatoes are sold on station platforms. Fruits and vegetables are deftly cut and beautifully presented, often wrapped in a banana leaf. Sugar cane juice is squeezed from huge roadside grinders straight into dubious-looking glasses. In the north, boiled eggs sprinkled with salt, pepper, and chopped cilantro are sold during winter evenings. *Chai* (tea) may be served in small clay cups that are dashed on the ground when finished. *Vada pav, pani puri, samosas, vada, jalebis,* and a vast array of other tasty snacks and sweets ensure that you can eat your way through the streets of India.

Regional Dishes

Geography and religion shape India's cuisine. Rice is the staple in the south and northeast, where rainfall is the heaviest. Delicious flat breads are the mainstay in the central plains and the north, where wheat is grown. Coastal peoples eat fish. Food preparation and ingredients in the northeast are heavily influenced by their neighbor, China, and often include pork. In Muslim-influenced areas, you can dig into Mughlai-style food characterized by thick, rich curries sprinkled with nuts and dried fruit. Gujarati cuisine is typically sweeter than other regions, since many Gujarati cooks add jaggery (brown sugar) to balance the salt. *Thali* is a common lunch in Tamil Nadu, comprising a huge stainless steel plate filled with rice and small bowls of *rasam* (pepper soup), *sambhar* (vegetable stew), *dhal* (lentils), yogurt, a sampling of several vegetable dishes, a *chapatti* or *puri*, and a dessert, and can be bought for a ridiculously low price. Andhra Pradesh is renowned for its fiery curries and the common practice of eating raw chilies as a side dish with rice.

Pickles are a necessity in Indian meals. The taste and type of pickle typically used varies not only regionally, but according to each home

India's sweets are worth sampling. Milk sweets— *gulab jamun* and *rasgulla*, *ras malai*, and *jalebis*—are the most common. Then there are regional or local specialties, such as *petha*—candied winter melon (Uttar

A selection of sweets prepared for the festival of Diwali.

Pradesh) and *payasam*—milk cooked with sugar, nuts, and noodles (Kerala). For special occasions, *ladoo* (sweet nut and chickpea balls) and sweets covered with edible silver leaf are served.

Chai or coffee may be served after dinner, though these are usually treated as something to offer before breakfast or in between meals. *Chai* is a delicious blend of milk, tea, and sugar brought to a boil. On special occasions and in some regions spices such as cinnamon, cloves, or ginger are added. Indians serve "milk coffee" made with "Nescafe" (instant coffee), milk, and plenty of sugar. You can find "filtered coffee" in south India. "Black coffee" means coffee with sugar, no milk.

FOOD CATEGORIES

Hot and Cold

If you're in India for any length of time, you will hear foods described as "hot" and "cold." This should not be mistaken for spicy and non-spicy or warm and chilled foods. It refers to a belief, rooted in Ayurvedic medicine, about how these types of food affect your body.

Hot foods should never be eaten by pregnant women because they can bring on a miscarriage. Eating papaya, especially the seeds, is believed to be a surefire way to abort. After the delivery of a baby, hot foods are required for recovery. They may include fruits and vegetables such as banana, pineapple, jackfruit, coconut, eggplant, and potatoes.

Meat, fish, eggs, nuts, and, predictably, red chilies are hot. Mangoes should be eaten in moderation, since they are "hot" enough to cause boils. Dairy products should be avoided by new mothers, since yogurt, buttermilk, and other "cold" dairy products will give your baby digestive problems. "Cold" foods cannot be eaten in winter without making you sick.

Other instructions you'll hear: do not drink water just before or during a meal; don't drink milk after eating something sour; don't eat ice cream or drink cold drinks when it's cold outside or when you have a cold. All of these dietary prohibitions are less well-known among the younger generations, but they may unthinkingly practice them since it is how their mothers and grandmothers raised them.

Clean and Unclean

There are other common food-related protocols that are in fact good practices for staying healthy in the Indian context. Nearly all Indians have "clean" and "unclean" foods. The most common "unclean" foods are all forms of meat for Hindus, pork for Muslims, and even for most Christians, and for some, shellfish.

Not just what one eats, but how, is important. The left hand is used for personal hygiene. The right hand only is used for serving and touching food. Left-handed children may have been trained to become right-handed. Left-handed foreigners are best advised to ask for a fork.

Alcohol

Drinking alcohol is still viewed in Indian society as a vice and the majority of Indians don't drink. Before Independence, Gandhi prompted local governments to outlaw liquor, and various levels of prohibition lasted until 1977. Gujarat, the northeast states, and, most recently, Kerala, are "dry" states. Nationally it is illegal to advertise alcohol; but Western influence, the rise of consumerism, and the changes in family structures and disposable income have encouraged an increase in drinking among young urban professionals and women. Alcohol consumption has doubled in the past decade.

Younger Indians can be found congregating in the many pub-style or chic restaurants that are growing in number and popularity all over urban India. The average drinking age is twenty-one, though it varies by state, ranging from eighteen in Rajasthan, to twenty-five in Delhi.

SPORTS AND OUT AND ABOUT

Indians are passionate about sports. Cricket and badminton top the charts for the number of people, not just professional athletes, who play.

India's ardor for sports and games is rooted in its history. During the Vedic period noblemen were competent in a variety of manly pursuits, including wrestling and hunting. Battle skills were turned into sports, becoming archery, discus throwing, weightlifting, and wrestling.

Wrestling in India is not so much a sport as a way of life. Men dedicate themselves to the disciplines and gurus required to learn the arts of *Pehlwani* (north India) or *Kalaripayat* (south).

Playing cricket on the Maidan, the largest urban park in Kolkata.

Martial art forms that were the precursors to judo and karate originated in India and spread to Asia with the Buddhist monks.

Parcheesi, chess, playing cards, and snakes and ladders, commonly known and played in the West, are ancient Indian board games.

Cricket

It is said that India has two religions: cricket and film. Although the official national sport is hockey, Indians have a passion for cricket, and the Board of Control for Cricket in India is the richest cricket board in the world. If there's a match going on, you can be sure that much of the country will be gathered around a TV, a radio, or plugged into their cell phones, cheering on their team.

Yoga

Self-realization in Hinduism requires an understanding of the physical and its relationship to the metaphysical. Yoga, meaning "union with Brahman," is a Hindu practice that has become a popular means of physical exercise in the West. It combines controlled breathing, specific postures, and withdrawal of the senses as a means of mastering the body and elevating the soul.

Kite Fighting

Kites are not just a child's plaything in India. Introduced by Chinese travelers, kite making and fighting are skills that have been passed on from father to son for centuries. *Patangs*—diamond-shaped bamboo and tissue paper constructions, maneuvered by a single

Young men preparing their kite for the festival of Raksha Bandham.

string—are the most common. Hundreds of these colorful tailless kites can be seen flying from rooftops during the festival of Raksha Bandhan (see page 15) and Independence Day. The aim is to cut the string of other kites, and to be the last kite flying. Ahmedabad's Kite Festival, held every January, draws kite fighters from around the world.

Out and About

India's terrain invites everything from snorkeling to skiing. But Indians are not typically nature buffs. Camping and hiking are not common pastimes, even though there are 104 national parks and more than 540 wildlife sanctuaries in the country. The greatest concentration are in the Andaman and Nicobar Islands.

The Himalayas stretch across the northern border of India. But you don't have to climb Mount Everest for spectacular views. A visit to Darjeeling or a hike up the hills around Nainital offer breathtaking vistas too.

The majority of Indians cannot swim. But people still picnic and play along India's many rivers, beautiful falls, and thousands of miles of coastline. Except in Goa and some of the more popular tourist beaches, Indian adults keep their clothes on, even if they venture into the water. If you plan to swim, be prepared to cover up and to be the center of attention no matter how you dress.

A FEW TOP SPOTS

There are so many cultural and natural attractions in India that it is worth mentioning a few spots that should not be missed.

North

Old and New Delhi are a "must." **Agra** is filled with architectural wonders, from the Taj Mahal and the Agra Fort to nearby Fatehpur Sikri (the City of Victory). **Varanasi** is the most holy Hindu place on the Ganges. **Sarnath** is the site of the Ashoka Pillar, where Buddha preached his first sermon. **Nainital** is one of many beautiful hill stations. Hike to see the Himalayas, go boating on the peaceful Naini Lake, or visit Sri Aurobindo Ashram (religious community). **Khajuraho** has Hindu temples and erotic sculptures. The Sikh Golden Temple in **Amritsar** is a spectacular historic site.

Lining up at the Kaziranga Elephant Festival in Assam.

East and Northeast

In **Kolkata**, you can visit Mother Teresa's Home for the Destitute and Dying; Kalighat Temple, where animal sacrifices are offered to the goddess Kali. On the Darjeeling Himalayan Railway, the "Toy Train" runs by steam from **Siliguri** to **Darjeeling**, with views of the Himalayas. In **Assam**, visit the Kaziranga National Park, which has the largest number of Indian rhinos and hosts the Elephant Festival.

South

Kochi (Cochin) has the famous Chinese fishing nets, Kerala backwaters, and the oldest Jewish settlement in India. **Madurai** has the Sri Meenakshi and Sundareswarar Temples, epitomizing South Indian Hindu architecture. **Cape Comorin**, or **Kanniyakumari**, is the southernmost tip of the Indian peninsula, where the Bay of Bengal, the Arabian Sea, and the Indian Ocean meet.

West

Rajasthan is filled with colorful cities. **Jodhpur**, known as the "blue city." In **Jaipur**, the beautiful "pink city," you can find Tiger Fort (Nahargah Fort) and **Udaipur**'s white palaces and lovely lakes and gardens. **Goa** has the best-known beaches, but don't miss the numerous wildlife sanctuaries and the Dudhsagar ("Milk Sea") Falls. The **Ellora Caves of Maharasthra**, the world's largest rock-hewn monastery, and **Ajanta Caves**, filled with ancient art, are UNESCO World Heritage Sites.

Safe Sightseeing

Buses, trains, and tour companies carry millions of people to India's famous historical, religious, and vacation spots. Interspersed with Indian tourists and pilgrims are foreign tourists and vacationing expats, conspicuous whether on a group tour bus or navigating trains and taxis on their own. You are likely to encounter unauthorized tour guides, beggars, pickpockets, and con artists.

Tour guides offer their services to individuals or small groups. Authorized guides should have identification, but badges can be faked. Often brochures provided at a historical site will give information about tours and tour guides, including fees. Don't give money in advance; don't allow anyone to hold your belongings, drag you into a souvenir shop, coerce you into taking a taxi to another site, or talk you into paying more at the end of the tour than was originally quoted. Those may all be indicators that you are being set up for theft, or worse. Dirty, smiling children may chat in English in a friendly

attempt to extract a few rupees from you. If you are
jostled on the street, your pocket has probably been
picked, as Indians avoid physical contact with others
except in the most crowded situations

CULTURAL ACTIVITIES

Religion and History
India is a paradise for those interested in religion or
history. Some religious celebration occurs nearly every
day, and there is no shortage of sacred sites and cities.
Five thousand years of recorded history make for
fascinating discoveries all over the country.

Delhi and Agra offer a wonderful introduction to
Mughal history, complete with famous forts and, of
course, the Taj Mahal. Cities famous for their temples
and spiritual history, such as Varanasi, Sarnath,
Bodhgaya, Haridwar, Amritsar, and Madurai, are
popular tourist destinations for Indians as well as for
foreigners.

Many of the holy places outside the more famous
tourist routes may have more restrictions and be less
tolerant of tourists. Should you wish to enter any
religious building, leave your shoes outside and, if you're
a woman, cover your head. If you are wearing shorts or
a sleeveless shirt (whether male or female), put off your
visit for another day when you are more appropriately
dressed. Some temples and mosques will not permit
anyone outside their religion to enter, so if you are not
a Hindu or Muslim check before you step inside.

The Taj Mahal was commissioned by the Mughal emperor Shah Jahan in 1632 to house the tomb of his beloved wife, Mumtaz Mahal.

If you keep your eyes open, you can spot India's smaller religious sites—its shrines. You may see them while crossing a bridge in south India, tucked under the base of a tree in north India, or on the crest of a hill in the mountain regions. Marked by a large, smooth stone or a carved statue, covered with garlands or snippets of marigolds, finger-painted with red powder or flanked by tiny oil candles, these sacred spots are home to gods, goddesses, saints, or spirits who are treated as local deities and worshiped and appeased. People come to these sites offering sweets and flowers, seeking protection or blessing. These shrines are often adjacent to temples of better-known deities.

The Arts
The richness and beauty of India's cultural diversity are manifest in its ancient architecture, paintings, music, dance, and craftsmanship, and its contemporary art, music, fashion, and cinema.

Music
For millennia the intensity, passion, devotion, and poetry of the Indian peoples have been poured into music. Both musician and listener become caught up in the experience, as all the senses are engaged by intricate sound patterns, rich color, exotic dance, clapping crowds, and pungent incense. For most foreigners the subtleties and beauty of India's classical music may require an adjustment of both mind and heart, which is the purpose and power of this music.

The tonal foundation for the composition of all of Indian classical and much of its contemporary music is the *raag* (Hindi) or *ragam* (Tamil), meaning "color" or "passion." A *raag* is a five-to-seven-note series used to form a melody. Unlike Western music, Indian classical music has no absolute pitch. The musician chooses a note from which all other notes follow. *Tal*—the rhythm—is the second necessary element. A third element—the "drone"—is usually played on a stringed instrument. The drone grounds the music, creating harmonics by plucking resonating notes that run through an entire song.

Improvisation is a unique aspect of Indian classical music. It is an art to be mastered through instruction, discipline, and secrets imparted by one's guru.

Much of India's music has been written to express religious devotion. *Bhajans* are simple, poetic songs or chants usually heard in, or near, temples and at religious events.

Ghazals, imported to India from Persia, can be spiritual songs, but are more often romantic recitations set to music.

Film songs (*filmi sangeet*) once made up the lion's share of India's music sales. Many were never even in a movie, but they became so popular that a separate genre label for the style came about. Indian pop music (Indipop) arose in the late 1970s and continues to spice up Indian classical and folk styles and remixes of film classics. In the 1990s, 70 percent of the music market was tied to film. But with the introduction of Indian rap and MTV India, all that changed. In the past few years, Indian hip-hop and rap artists have ascended from their underground status to become the fastest growing genre for streaming in India. "Desi hip-hop," the musical child birthed from the Indian Diaspora, speaks to the shifts in identity (race, gender, and culture) that are taking place globally.

Technological change has also affected Indian music, which has gone digital, providing more than 91 percent of the revenue of the recorded music industry. India is the second-largest smartphone market in the world, and one of its biggest music markets is ringtones.

Dance
Vocals and instruments are often accompanied by dance. Traditionally, eight regional dance forms have been

accepted in India as "classical." But this number is growing, along with the number of states and the rise in linguistic-based nationalism. *Kathak*, meaning "storyteller," developed in northern India during the Mughal period and was originally performed by courtesans in the courts of kings. *Kathakali* (Kerala) tells the stories of the Hindu epics, *Ramayana* and *Mahabharata*, and the ancient *Puranas. Manipuri* (Manipur) depicts tales of the life of Lord Vishnu. *Sittriya* (Assam) is a fifteenth-century dance form honoring Vishnu. *Mohiniaattam* (Kerala) is the dance of Vishnu's enchanting female avatar, Mohini. *Sattriya Kuchipudi* (Andhra Pradesh), uniquely characterized by movement combined with speech, dramatizes Hindu mythology. *Odissi* (Orissa) is the oldest Indian classical dance. Carvings of *Odissi* dancers can be found on the

Hand gestures (*mudras*) convey the story and feelings of the characters portrayed.

Sun Temple at Konark. *Odissi* and *Bharatanatyam* (Tamil
Nadu) are the only two classical forms considered "temple
dances." They were historically performed by *devadasis*—
young girls who served priests and entertained the elite,
having been given by their families in "marriage" to a
god. Other dance forms include *Bihu* (Assam), *Bhangra*
(Punjab), and *Perini Shivatandavam* (Telengana).

There are myriad forms of folk dance, many of which
are still performed during religious and seasonal festivals
as well as for special community occasions. Colorful
costumes, traditional headdresses, or jewelry add swirl
and sparkle to these local and tribal dances.

Movies

Cinema is one of India's most renowned art forms. As
many as two thousand movies in more than twenty
languages are cranked out annually, and not all of them
from Bollywood. There is a rise in regional filmmaking
and a diversification into the international market, from
the US to China. Nearly a third of Indian movies are now
filmed in North America. With volume that high, it's no
wonder that a majority are based on standard formulae:
boy loves girl from afar, boy meets girl, tragedy strikes,
and either love overcomes all or no one lives happily
ever after. Of course there is always song and dance,
sometimes when you least expect it. But that can be
what makes Hindi movies entertaining, even if you
don't understand the language.

Worthy films should not get lost in the crowd. Hindi,
Tamil, Bengali, Kannada, Malayalam, Marathi, and Telugu
cinema continue to produce acclaimed works. *The Apu*

Trilogy, three Bengali films directed by Satyajit Ray in the late 1950s, won numerous awards, and these are recognized to be among the best movies of all time.

Not all films are based on original scripts. Many are not-so-cloaked remakes of classic movies or stories from the West. *Black* (2005) is partially based on Helen Keller's story. Films based on Jane Austen novels are popular: *Bride and Prejudice* (2004) is an entertaining version of the Jane Austen novel; *Aisha* (2010) is India's version of *Emma*; and *Kandukondain Kandukondain* (2000) is a Tamil adaptation of *Sense and Sensibility*. Remakes of more recent American movies include *The Godfather* (1972) as *Sarkar* (2005); *Hitch* (2005) as *Partner* (2007); *Three Men and a Baby* (1987) as *Heyy Babyy* (2007); *Rain Man* (1988) as *Yubbraj* (2008); and the 1982 blockbuster, *Rambo* as *Rambo* (2018).

In India, both theaters and theatergoers have changed over the past few years, and Indian movies are changing in response. Multiplex cinemas have replaced single-screen movie houses. Satellite TV and the Internet have opened the door to other kinds of big- and small-screen productions. An increase in income and leisure time among the middle class has been a boon to the movie industry. What was previously a place for young males to congregate once a month has now become respectable for a weekly family outing.

At the end of the twentieth century, big-budget productions took a dive. Finding it less feasible to finance the requisite song and dance routines, the film industry looked for a solution. They found it in English and export.

In the 1980s and '90s many English films were made; but the themes were still standard *masala* (typical Bollywood fare). Over the past decades, increasing numbers of movies are being made in English and Hinglish—a linguistic and cultural mix of Hindi and English. These films, often produced or directed by NRIs (nonresident Indians), express the personal identity, generational conflicts, social struggles, and range of emotions of Indians swept up in a massive culture shift. Films such as *Monsoon Wedding* (2001), *Namesake* (2006), *Slumdog Millionaire* (2008), *English Vinglish* (2012), and *The Extraordinary Journey of the Fakir* (2018) entertain as well as educate Westerners in traditional Indian cultural themes and contemporary shifts.

Should you take in a movie while in India, prepare to enjoy a community experience. Talking throughout, cell phones ringing, cheering on the hero, or singing along would not be considered rude or unusual. So go with the flow and have fun. It is all part of the India experience.

Indian shops, inside and outside the country, carry plenty of DVDs, many of them pirated. Eighty million pirated DVDs are sold every year. You can usually spot them by the grainy printing of the covers. Antipiracy laws do exist. Those who breach them in India can face up to three years in prison and a fine of up to 200,000 rupees (US $2,800)—twice the average per capita income. But in reality most offenders get away with paying only a small fine, and go back to making more illegal copies.

Literature

The Hindu epics and other Sanskrit scriptures, originally sung or recited in order to transmit them from one generation to the next, are fascinating literary works, regardless of your religious beliefs. Ancient poetry, such as the twelfth-century *Gitagovinda* ("The Cowherd's Song") and the works of the fourteenth-century poets Tulasidas and Kabir Das, are still known and recited.

Though many think of Sanskrit as the primary literary language, classical literature has been written in all of India's languages. Tamil predates Sanskrit, beginning in the first century CE. A. K. Ramanujan is famous for translating Tamil classics into English. Gandhi wrote his autobiography, *My Experiments with Truth*, 1929, in Gujarati. Bengali was the language of Rabindranath Tagore, who was awarded the Nobel Prize for Literature in 1913. He composed more than 2,200 songs, including India's national anthem. His unique adaptation of Indian classical and folk music led to the emergence of a new genre: Rabindra Sangeet. His music, poetry, and perspective shaped not only Indian music, but also its history and culture.

In the post-British era, English has been a recognized medium of classic Indian literature, too. R. K. Narayan writes of south Indian village life. Mulk Raj Anand's novels are social protest. Salman Rushdie became infamous overnight with the publication of *The Satanic Verses*. Arundhati Roy and Aravind Adiga both won the Booker Prize: Roy for *The God of Small Things* and Adiga for *The White Tiger*. Anita Desai, author of *The ZigZag Way*, is known for her powerful portrayal of her central female

characters. *A Suitable Boy* by Vikram Seth tells the story
of four families who must navigate post-partition politics,
religious conflicts, and social change.

SHOPPING FOR PLEASURE

Since 2002, the number of malls has grown from nine to
more than six hundred. Some of the larger ones mimic
those of Dubai, featuring indoor skiing, water parks,
and gondola rides. Still, most Indians continue to shop
out of necessity rather than as a pastime. In traditional
markets, goods of a similar nature are sold by rows of
shopkeepers in the same vicinity. You go to the spice
market for spices, the fish market for fish, the gold *gully*
(lane) for gold, and the plastic lane for buckets and
boxes.

If shopping is your interest, you will find more
than enough to occupy your time. Each region has its
own specialty. Rajasthan offers mirror-work hangings,
papier-mâché puppets, traditional shoes with curled
toes, jewelry, and antique furniture. Sandalwood soaps,
incense, and carvings are famous in Karnataka. Varanasi
and Chennai are both known for silk, and Kashmir
for embroidered shawls and clothing. Unique fabrics,
classical instruments, Darjeeling teas, and spices are other
items you might want to take home. You can buy them
locally or find everything in Delhi's excellent emporiums.

Shopping hours and closed days are variable
depending on the religious beliefs of the shop owners,
holidays celebrated, and family needs and circumstances.

The Shopping Experience

A woman's first priority in India may be to find a tailor who can "stitch" the latest in *shalwar-kameez* fashion. Cotton, "terry-cot" (cotton-polyester blend), or silk outfits can be made to suit style, figure, and purse. Ready-made clothes are also available.

While shopping you may encounter the Indian unwillingness to say "no." To say "no" to you is to lose his reputation as well as a relationship with you as a customer. Some shopkeepers will try all manner of dodges, expecting you to understand that they do not have what you're asking for. It's your responsibility as the customer to get the message. They may try to sell you something else. You might be told to "come back tomorrow." (If you do, it will still not be there.) Or, if you're lucky, he'll say, "Wait one minute." In a few minutes, he'll reappear with what you want, having run down the street to find it at another store.

Bargaining

In malls and larger stores prices are fixed. But elsewhere most shopkeepers expect you to bargain. However, you should only begin the process if you truly intend to buy. You can get a feel for prices by visiting other stores first. However, you will still be charged more than the locals, so try to take an Indian friend with you and let him or her do the talking. You'll save some money and get a bit of training on how to improve your own bargaining skills for the next time.

Look at several things, and ask the shopkeeper about them. When you find what you want, don't seem too interested. Ask the cost, and say, "Is that your best price?" He will suggest slightly less. You can then say, "Oh, that's too much!" He may ask, "What will you pay?" State a figure that is half or even a third of the original price, intending to pay a little more. If he refuses, move toward the door. He will probably come down a little, you go up a little, and carry on until you reach a price acceptable to you both. Don't leave unless you're willing to lose your find. If you return, he'll ask the full price. In some places you can pay less than half the asking price, especially if you're buying in quantity, or if you're the first customer of the day (considered auspicious). But abusing this by suggesting a ridiculous price will only generate ill will. So keep it light and fun, and remember that they're trying to make a living.

Exchanging Money

Because of the hassle and expense of exchanging money, it may be in your best interest to change a large amount in the airport at the start of your journey. US dollars and British pounds are the easiest to exchange. You can use credit and debit cards in major cities; ATMs and foreign-exchange kiosks can be found in many places; but using rupees is trouble free. If there is a power outage or your credit cards are lost or stolen, you will need cash.

A word of warning: there are many unauthorized money changers. For your protection, don't exchange money with anyone who approaches you on the street. Use airport exchange services or a bank. Banking hours are 10:00 a.m. to 2:00 p.m., Monday through Friday. Expect to wait in line, and have your passport ready.

CHAPTER SEVEN

TRAVEL, HEALTH, & SAFETY

India's got it all: planes, trains, buses, taxis, cars, scooters, camels, elephants, bullock carts, horse-drawn *tongas*, along with auto, cycle, and human rickshaws. The rapid growth of the economy since the early 1990s has been matched by ever-growing demands on the transportation infrastructure and services. Though travel within the country is relatively inexpensive, poor roads, an aging railway system, chaotic airports, and a general lack of order and sanitation make it a challenge. The government is working to improve national highways, rural roads, and road maintenance. The World Bank is also investing heavily in road and rail upgrades, and airports are being privatized in order to make headway on the ground and in the air.

Navigating India's transportation options as well as looking after yourself and your property during your travels will require effort. But equipped with the right information, a good attitude, and a willingness to ask for help, traveling itself will be an unforgettable and even treasured part of your stay in India.

VISAS

In 2014, India introduced an e-Visa upon arrival system. Now citizens of 166 countries can apply online for an e-Visa. Multiyear tourist visas are available for those applying in advance through a visa service or consulate. Because visa laws change frequently, it's best to contact the Indian Consulate General for the latest information.

ARRIVAL

Brace yourself for impact when arriving in India. The sensory overload of crowd, sound, and smell can cause even experienced travelers to question their skills and their sanity. Airports are chaotic.

Stepping outside, the heat hits you like a wave. You will be engulfed in a swarm of taxi-*walas* vying for your business. Scruffy-looking children tug on your sleeve, looking for a handout. The smell of pollution tinged with urine is overwhelming, the decibel level is deafening, and the full assault on body and mind can be exhausting, making it hard to think. For this reason, some decisions about what to do next should be made ahead of time: advance preparation will alleviate some of the stress you'll encounter on arrival in India.

AIR TRAVEL

India has twenty international airports, and eighty functioning domestic airports. The government-owned Indian Airlines had a monopoly until 2005, when private companies were allowed to operate. Competition has fueled better fares and services, and flying within the country has become very affordable. With the rise in private airlines, air travel volume continues to escalate. This is good for those wishing to go to more places faster, but India's airports lack the infrastructure to handle this growing demand. According to the Center for Asia Pacific Aviation, air travel demands will outstrip airport capacity in the next few years without enormous investments in infrastructure and airplanes.

BY ROAD

India has the second largest roadway system in the world, including 228 national highways, 3.6 million miles (5.8 million km) of roads, with 125,000 miles (200,000 km) more to be laid down by 2022. Roads still carry 90 percent of the travelers and 65 percent of the freight in India. While the number of roads has increased, road quality has not. By and large, they are poorly made and maintained, narrow, and congested. According to the World Bank only 20 percent of India's roads are in a decent condition.

Taxis

Prepaid taxis are the safest way to go from the airport
or railway station to your hotel or guesthouse.
You will be assured of a legitimate driver and the
standard fare—visible on the meter. While tipping is
not necessary, a small fee per item of luggage may be
added on to the fare. Ask at the prepaid counter.

Newer cars have invaded taxi territory. But most
cabs are still the yellow or yellow and black Premier
Padminis and Hindustan Ambassadors, both made
since the mid-1950s and not air-conditioned. The
company making Premier Padminis went out of
business in the late 1990s, but these old cars are still
the reliable rulers of India's roads. Slogans painted
along the top of each taxi—"*Allah hu Akbar,*" "*Ram
Satya Nam,*" or "Jesus is Lord"—advertise the driver's
religious affiliation. Inside the taxi you'll see his
family photos pinned to the visor, small pictures of
his gods or religious symbols on the window or glued
to the dashboard, and religious paraphernalia meant
to ward off the evil eye hanging from the rearview
mirror. While you're looking around, note the
driver's name and ID number on his posted license,
in the unlikely event that you encounter a problem.

En route, the driver may tell you that he can't find
your hotel or that it's fully booked, and will offer to
take you to a different hotel. It's a scam. If he insists
he doesn't know the place, tell him to take you back
to the prepaid counter to get another taxi. Do not
give him the receipt you received from the prepaid
counter until he sets you down at your desired

destination or takes you back to where you came from. That receipt ensures he gets paid.

Most cab drivers in the major cities speak enough English to understand your destination and tell you how much you owe, though the meter will show you the fare, too. Some drivers might offer to give you a tour of the city en route to your destination. If they've been especially helpful or appropriately friendly, feel free to give them a tip.

Taxis can be hired on a regular basis to drive you to work or school, or while you're visiting a city as a tourist. In general, they can be relied on to show up at the right time and get you where you want to go without difficulty. A taxi driver may ask if he can pick up other passengers on the way. While this is a common practice, for your safety and peace of mind it's perfectly all right to decline.

Auto Rickshaws and Ridesharing

Cheaper and more maneuverable than taxis, India's yellow and black auto rickshaws are ubiquitous. Doorless, three-wheel cabs on a motorcycle engine, these tiny vehicles have been known to carry a dozen people. They offer no protection from pollution in congested traffic. Carry a handkerchief or light scarf to wrap around your nose and mouth and enjoy the up close and personal views afforded by this fun mode of transportation. For those with asthma or other health concerns, they may not be the best choice.

Uber and other ridesharing options, such as Ola (in city) or BlaBlacar (intercity) are increasingly

A cycle and auto rickshaw in New Delhi.

available in major cities, providing another inexpensive alternative to taxis.

Driving

India's auto industry is expanding rapidly, with more than 230 million cars on the road and growing annually. More than two million were sold in 2017. Tata, Hindustan Motors, and Maruti, India's main manufacturers, have been joined by Ford, Honda, Fiat, MG Motors, Kia, and others looking for a share of the market. Even so, only about 5 percent of Indian families own a car.

Driving is best left to the Indians, but you can rent a car, with or without a driver, in any major city. There are official rules and regulations posted by the Department of Road Transport and Highways, and you should be aware of these. Driving is on the left side of the road.

With some exceptions, roads are narrow and riddled with potholes. Cows and dogs may share the road, even in cities. Center lines or lane markers do not mean much, and any gap is a possible "lane." Turn signals are rare. Horns blare. Policemen may direct traffic at a junction even with a working stoplight, simply because lights may be ignored. Expect to find yourself in a knot of traffic at some time during your travels that will require the untangling expertise of a few fearless men.

Should you be involved in an accident or stopped for some reason by the police, severe fines and/or imprisonment could be in store—though a reasonable bribe will probably not be declined.

Although public transportation systems are at least adequate throughout India, you may want to hire a car with a driver if you'd like to go at your own pace or get to a remote spot without the inevitable crowds and delays of bus travel or the geographic restrictions of a taxi. Hiring a car and driver is relatively inexpensive and will still provide enough thrills to suit any adrenalin junkie. Or take BlaBlacar, a ridesharing option that uses Facebook for sign-ins, to find others going in your direction who can offer you a lift.

Buses
Buses are a cheap way to travel, but you get what you pay for: constant stops, cramped seats, bumpy roads, and no "facilities" either on the bus or at bus stations.

City buses are overcrowded, chaotic, and dirty. Everyone pushes and shoves to get inside, and it's often impossible to maneuver enough elbow room to take change from your pocket to pay the fare. Sometimes the conductor can't even get through. When that happens you pass your fare to the conductor via other passengers.

Pickpockets invisibly conduct their business in the press of the crowd. Women standing in the aisles may be groped and must figure out how to defend themselves against pickpockets and perverts.

City buses may not always come to a complete halt. If you hesitate to jump off at your stop, the oncoming crowds may push you back inside the bus, where you'll be stuck until you work up the nerve to press through again to the door and fling yourself off at the next stop.

Long-distance buses often show nonstop films and videos, not all of them suitable for children. At bus stations, vendors of all ages jump on to sell cold drinks, *chai*, and snacks. Beggars rush to the windows asking for money or food. If you need to get off the bus, check with the driver first. Ask him to wait for you to return, or you may find yourself stranded without your luggage. Women's bathroom facilities are few and far between.

A few Rapid Transit systems are working to improve buses and their services, including the addition of new buses and air-conditioning.

Pedestrians

The most difficult thing you may be required to do while in India is cross the road. Pedestrians do not have the right of way. When there is a space in the traffic, head for the middle of road and wait again while cars, scooters, autos, and buses speed past. Your safest course of action is to wriggle your way into the middle of a crowd and go with the flow.

Accidents

India sadly leads the world in road-related fatalities. Currently eighteen people die every hour. Speeding, drunk driving, disregard for seat belts, or helmets, and poor road design and maintenance are the main factors. Perhaps the recent US $500 million loan from the World Bank to the Indian government for the construction of 4,350 miles (7,000 km) "all-weather roads" in rural areas will help make a difference.

Aggression is increasingly part of the driving experience. Road rage accounts for 10 percent of the country's murders. Irritation, shouting, and gesturing mount, especially during the hot season. Do not respond in kind. Though it rarely happens to foreigners, mobs have been known to exact a justice of their own. So don't get out of your car if confronted by an angry driver, even if there has been an injury (whether you caused it or not). Solicit the help of people from the crowd that will inevitably gather to calm the aggressor and to give you advice.

BY RAIL

Asia's largest rail system, the government-owned Indian Railways, has nearly 40,000 miles (64,000 km) of track woven through the whole of India. Around thirteen thousand trains carry over twenty-three thousand passengers per day. Kolkata, Lucknow, Delhi, Jaipur, Mumbai, Bengaluru, Kochi, Chennai, and Hyderabad all have metro systems, with more being developed elsewhere. Although flying has become very affordable, rail travel is a fascinating way to experience India.

Class Options
There are several classes of rail travel, though not all are available on every train.

Second Class (Unreserved)
For a close encounter with "the real India" this is the place to be. No reservation is required to travel second class. Coaches are divided into multiple compartments, each designed to seat six people, but traveling without a reservation means that as many people as possible squeeze in. As a foreigner traveling in Second Class, you will be an attraction, adding to the number of people who desire to sit as close to you as possible. Compartments have an aisle, beyond which is another seat meant for two. Don't choose a seat on the aisle, as constant traffic means that your feet and luggage are in the way and your belongings are an easy target for thieves.

Third Class (Unreserved)
People fill every possible space, with more entering the train at every station, requiring you to move over, take up even less room, and be even more alert about watching your belongings. The uncomfortable wooden seats and

the cramped conditions make long-distance travel in this class something you may want to avoid.

Sleeper Class

While still crowded, noisy, and not so clean, Sleeper Class requires reservations, assuring travelers of a padded seat during the day and a berth at night. Each coach has multiple compartments, each with six berths and two additional berths along the aisle, making for close traveling companions. If you have the misfortune to book an aisle berth, you'll discover at night when you put your "bed" down that it is enclosed at both ends, making it considerably shorter than the ones in the six-person section. In the compartment, center berths are folded up against the wall during the day to allow relatively comfortable seating. Unless you've reserved the upper berth that remains down twenty-four hours a day, don't expect to stretch your legs or be able to take a midday nap.

Air-Conditioned: 3A, 2A, 1A

Three Tiered Air-Conditioned Class (3A) has sealed, tinted windows, extra padded berths, and, of course, air-conditioning. Compartments here are also open, but the train car itself is locked at night and protected by the conductor, who makes sure that no unauthorized vendors or passengers enter. A sheet, a thin woolen blanket, and a pillow are provided, as are meals, if you have reserved them at the time you purchased your ticket.

Two Tiered Air-Conditioned Class (2A) is the same as 3A, but with only four berths per compartment and two along the aisle. Curtains can be pulled across your berth, giving privacy at night as you sleep.

First-Class Air-Conditioned Class (1A) tickets costs as much as an air fare. Unlike all the other options, each two- or four-berth compartment is closed with a door that can be locked from the inside. There are no aisle berths.

Some day trains have AC Chair Cars, which is like economy air travel. Because they are air-conditioned and relatively cheap, they're a better option for many than second class. Toilets tend to be cleaner in all of the AC classes. The only downside to traveling AC occurs if the train breaks down en route. Then you're stuck in a closed car with windows that cannot be opened.

In most of these classes, don't be surprised to have to wrestle your way on to the train only to find someone else in your assigned seat. People usually wait for the boarding chaos to die down before adjusting themselves into the right spaces. If you have a problem with someone who refuses to leave your seat or who says they have the same seat, simply wait for the conductor to come and resolve it.

Ladies Only

Commuters jostle for space. For women it's often an unpleasant, if not humiliating, experience. In response to this need, many suburban trains have "Ladies' Compartments." These are often located at either end of a train, and may be hard to find and harder to enter, especially during morning rush hours. It's not uncommon for men to force their way into compartments marked "Ladies only" to find a seat or to harass, molest, or rob female passengers. There are also complaints made about *hijras* (eunuchs) feeling free to sit in the ladies' section. Many local and all long-distance trains have "ladies' special" cars for women only. Well-lit, brightly painted coaches have been designed for the comfort and security of working women and students, with five female constables and three male officers on patrol. Recently Jaipur turned one of its stations into an all-woman station, with women in every position from ticket counter clerks to security. Don't worry. Men are allowed to travel to and from there.

DOS AND DON'TS OF HARASSMENT

If you are harassed on a train:
- Don't expect a polite verbal rebuke to solve the problem.
- Do enlist help from a man traveling with a wife or family.
- Don't assume you've done anything wrong.
- Do tell train officials immediately. Ask to register the incident in the official complaint book.
- Do appreciate that the vast majority are decent men, who will treat you with respect and come to your aid in a fatherly or brotherly fashion.

Reservations
Reservations can be made in advance for all classes of accommodation: via the Internet (expect technical

problems), at a station (expect long lines), or through a travel agent (expect a small fee). Reservations are not required for second or third class. Ladies-only lines are usually available. Look for the sign, or a line of women only.

Train timetables may be difficult to read, and station names are not city names. Prices for the same destination may vary, based on travel time or route. Passenger trains can be very slow, stopping at every station; express trains are twice as fast, but require reservations made weeks in advance. Don't be shy about asking for help to decipher timetables, posted information, or the system.

RAC or "Reservation Against Cancellation" means that you've been placed on a waiting list for a sleeper berth. (It is not the same as "Wait Listed," which simply means you're waiting for an RAC.) Arrive at the station early to find the passenger list on the reservation board. If your name is on the list, you have a seat, though this does not assure you of a berth. Do not get on a train for an overnight journey without a reservation. There will probably be no berth or seat available. You can be put off the train or forced to stand or sit outside the toilet at the end of the car. Not only is it uncomfortable, it's unsafe.

Tourist Counters and Quotas
At larger stations there will be a separate tourist office where only foreigners are allowed to book tickets in air-conditioned comfort with people who can answer any questions. You may need to pay in cash to buy a ticket in the tourist office. Cash payments will require

your passport and US dollars, British pounds sterling, or rupees if you can show a bank receipt for exchange transactions. Trains are typically full, so whenever possible, book in advance. But there is a tourist quota, making it occasionally possible to find a berth even during peak months or in an emergency. If there is no tourist office, ask to speak with the person in charge of the station—usually the Station Superintendent or the Station Master. They have the power to sell you Tourist, VIP, or Emergency Quota tickets when available.

Luggage and *Sahayaks* (Coolies)

Luggage allowance on trains is similar to that on airlines. How much you can take depends on your ticket class, so be sure to ask about it when you purchase your ticket. Overweight baggage will cost you dearly. *Sahayaks* wearing red shirts and badges are available to carry your luggage at every railway station. They will approach you with a smile and offer to carry your bags for an exorbitant price. If you want one to put your bags on the train (rather than just on the platform), establish this up front. After a bit of haggling, he may pick up your bags, telling you to pay whatever you wish, but don't hand them over until you have agreed upon a price. It's worth a few rupees to have the expert help. He will lock them under the seat for you if you have a chain and lock handy.

Always lock your luggage under the seat on an overnight train trip. Before your destination, the conductor will alert you to prepare to disembark. Or ask other passengers to tell you when you're nearing the station. That is the time to unlock your luggage, gather your belongings and your ticket, and move toward the door. As you enter the station, coolies will spot you and run to help you get your luggage down, and find a taxi.

It is possible to check in your bags at the start of your train trip. They will be put in a separate baggage compartment and unloaded at your destination for you to collect at the designated baggage office. It is, however, best to take them with you on the train, even though it seems like a hassle. The wait and the possible bribe required to collect them are rarely worth the "convenience" of checking them in, unless you have excess baggage that will not fit under your seat.

On the Train

Train journeys between north and south can take three or more days. It's three days well spent if you're interested in culture or language learning, enjoying the landscape, or simply want a very Indian experience.

At every station, unless you're in an AC or women's carriage that is locked or guarded, the aisles will fill up with Indian Railway approved *chai-walas* and snack vendors. It's a good idea to carry small bills and change for any items you wish to purchase. If at a station you want to get off to buy a snack, check with someone to make sure the train stops long enough for you to disembark, make your purchase, and still make it back on the train.

Ticket holders for overnight journeys can buy meals onboard. Check at the station when you purchase your ticket or with the conductor once you're on the train.

Basic vegetarian meals are served. Soon after departure, someone will take your order for dinner and for breakfast the next morning. There are no dining cars. Meals are brought to you in your compartment. Don't expect to sit up late. After dinner, everyone will retire. If you don't get the hint, you will be asked politely to stand up while people lower their berths and adjust their bedding.

You may find yourself the only woman in an all-male compartment or occupying a berth across the aisle from a person of the opposite sex. In this country, where privacy is not an issue, no one thinks anything of it.

Expect to be awoken early by the *chai-wala* asking if you'd like hot milk coffee or *chai*. People will head for the bathrooms in the early morning to wash and brush their teeth before taking food.

Using the toilet on a train is an experience. Squatting over a hole with a view of the speeding tracks is motivation to use the handrail. But if you've never used one, you'd better practice before taking a train trip. Extra dexterity and strength are required to balance on a moving train. Toilet use is not allowed at stations; nevertheless, some stations have sweepers working full-time on the tracks to clear waste.

Although Indian Railways is working to keep all but authorized passengers and vendors off their trains, others do manage to enter. Children or adults sweep up compartment floors, asking for "tips." Performers sing or dance in the aisles, hoping to be paid for entertaining. Pickpockets and thieves find a way in, too. Keep documents and cash concealed on your person at all times. If someone new appears to be eyeing you or your luggage, say something to the people with whom you're traveling and point out the person to the conductor. At night, keep your head, your jewelry, and any small bags away from open windows. Thieves standing on the platform have been known to reach through the window bars to pull earrings out of pierced ears.

In the midst of crowds and necessary cautions, don't miss the people. The vast majority of Indians are respectful, hospitable, and helpful. You'll find them to be delightful and intelligent travel companions.

HEALTH

India's Health
Despite decades of effort and education by both government and nonprofit sectors, huge strides in India's economy and technology, and the popularity of medicine as a profession, India is sadly the world's leader in child malnutrition, diabetes, tuberculosis, and typhoid.

It seems impossible for infrastructures to keep pace with population. Good health care remains inaccessible for India's majority. According to the Gates Foundation, 66 percent of Indians who died with treatable problems, died due to the poor quality of the care they received. Bad water, improper waste management, and air pollution result in over 2.5 million deaths each year. Low child immunization, increased travel, and overprescribing of antibiotics all contribute to the spread of communicable diseases.

In contrast, India has some excellent hospitals and highly qualified doctors, but staff and facilities are forced to work beyond their capacity as people seeking medical care pour in from distant villages or neighboring states where care is absent. Poor pay, poorly maintained hospitals and clinics, lack of advancement opportunity, and corruption discourage good doctors and nurses from providing care in needy rural areas and have pushed many of India's finest physicians to practice medicine outside India.

Even where health care is available, poverty and misconceptions about disease or healing prevent many people from going to doctors. Understanding of basic health issues such as proper nutrition or treating diarrhea is often derived from folk beliefs and remedies. Only 20 percent of the entire population carries health insurance. In 2018 Modi rolled out "affordable health care" to remedy this. *Ayushman Bharat*, "bless India with long and healthy life", offers health insurance for the poor and the promise of wellness clinics around the country.

Medication can be had over the counter without a doctor's prescription, so many poor people self-diagnose or rely on their corner pharmacist for medical advice.

India's Medicine

A majority of people in India turn to the naturopathic Ayurvedic system of medicine to meet their basic medical needs. Ayurveda (Sanskrit, "life science") arose in India during the Vedic period and is written about in the ancient Hindu scriptures, the *Vedas*. Ayurveda defines health as balance, illness as imbalance. The three bodily energies, or *doshas* ("that which deteriorates"), of air, fire, and water can be set in order through eating foods based on body type, proper digestion, physical exercise, and yoga or meditation.

Siddha medicine is another popular system from Tamil Nadu. The Hindu god Shiva is said to have passed down the rules of proper balance of the three energies to his followers ("*siddhar,*" those with extraordinary power), which cover dietary restrictions, the use of herbs, plants, metals, minerals, and chemicals, yoga, and meditation.

Homeopathy, a German form of alternative medicine, is also widely practiced in India.

Most of India's hospitals, unlike the West, are multidisciplinary, utilizing these various forms of medicine to treat their patients. Perhaps this, along with the inexpensive costs, for Westerners, of medical treatment, is why India is becoming a destination for medical tourism.

Sanitation

The signs of India's sanitation problems can be seen—and smelled—everywhere. Trash and refuse are nonchalantly disposed of, handled only by certain low or outcaste groups of people. Wandering cows, bulls, and goats serve as a cleanup crew, too, eating rotting vegetables tossed near the market. Pigs search side streets for human waste.

Public lavatories are not always available when you need one. Men merely need to find a wall, but women will find the lack of facilities difficult. In major cities it's best to look for a hotel or restaurant. Make use of clean places when you find them.

Food and Water

Many parasites, bacteria, and diseases, including hepatitis and typhoid (India's most common communicable disease), are waterborne. The easiest way to protect your health is by drinking only bottled water or bringing your own filter. Don't drink tap water or anything served with ice. When buying bottled water or soft drinks, check the cap to make sure it has not been previously opened. It's not uncommon for shopkeepers or *dhabbah-walas* to refill used bottles with tap water or homemade "soft drinks." Fruit juice may contain unfiltered water. So ask before ordering, or simply avoid them altogether. Use bottled water to brush your teeth, or brush without water.

It's not just ingested water that can make you sick. Pollution from water and food is more common during the monsoon. If you're in India at that time, beware of waterborne diseases. Rivers may not be safe to swim in. After heavy rain, streets will be flooded with dirty water. If you have to walk in flooded streets, bathe or dry off as soon as possible. Mosquitoes breed in standing water, which becomes a source of serious diseases, such as malaria and dengue fever. The high humidity in most of India promotes fungal growth on walls in homes and public buildings. Those suffering from asthma will need to take extra precautions and have their inhalers or medication on hand.

There are common rituals and protocols observed in daily life that promote purity and, in fact, are good practices for staying healthy in the Indian context. As we have seen, nearly all Indians have clean and unclean foods. Even if you don't share their beliefs, these food restrictions have developed for a reason. Cooked vegetarian food is always the safest choice when you're eating out. Meat may not be fresh, especially if eating in bus or train stations.

Diarrhea, or "loose motion," is the most common problem for visitors to India. Make sure you drink plenty of clean water or fresh coconut water (in the shell). An Indian specialty, lime soda, made with either sugar or salt, is good for rehydration. Yogurt and *kichirdi* (rice cooked with lentils) can also help. You may want to seek local medical attention. Your doctor can prescribe antibiotics for you to take with you on your trip, or you can buy them over the counter once you're in India.

Heat
The heat can affect you before you know it. To prevent heat exhaustion, cramps, or stroke, stay hydrated and stay indoors, limiting physical activity during the hot season. Heatstroke, which can be fatal, is characterized by increased body temperature, flushed skin, disorientation, and sometimes hallucinations and seizures. It requires immediate medical attention. See the Centers for Disease Control and Prevention (https://www.cdc.gov) for details regarding self-care in India's extreme temperatures.

HIV/AIDS
Though HIV affects people on every level of society, it remains a critical issue for the high-risk populations of prostitutes, truck drivers and other migrant workers,

drug users, and those engaging in male homosexual activity.

India has the third largest incidence of HIV in the world; however, new cases of HIV/AIDS have decreased by 46 percent, and AIDS-related deaths by 22 percent, since 2010, thanks to education, the radical increase of testing sites, the rise in availability of treatment, and many other measures by the government, the medical community, and human rights groups.

Be Prepared

Before traveling to India, check on immunization requirements and recommendations at least six months in advance. You may need a series of injections over an extended period.

Make sure you carry your insurance information and phone numbers for your physician, an emergency contact back home, and a contact number in India, if possible. Find more information on current health risks and prevention at the Centers for Disease Control and Prevention (opposite) and the World Health Organization (http://www.who.int/en).

SAFETY

Violence

Terror attacks, bombings, and kidnappings, sometimes targeting Westerners, are front-page news. Jammu Kashmir and the border between India and Pakistan have ongoing disputes that make travel to those places dangerous. Most of India's tensions are between castes or religious groups, including more recent anti-Christian and anti-Muslim violence. The US State Department (http://travel.state.gov/) provides up-to-date information and travel warnings; as do the British Foreign and Commonwealth Office (http://www.fco.gov.uk); and the Canadian Foreign Affairs and International Trade (http://www.voyage.gc.ca).

Restricted Areas

The Indian government requires special permission to visit certain parts of India, including the Andaman and Nicobar Islands, Lakshadweep (the Union Territory of the Laccadives Islands), many northeastern states, and some border regions.

Crime

Pickpocketing is common in and around tourist sites and public transportation. Keep valuables, documents, and cash hidden on your person, and tuck cameras in a theft-proof bag when not in use. Don't leave valuables in your hotel room. Put them in the hotel's safe, if it has one. As a foreigner you're an easy target for theft.

Some foreigners, eager to trust people, unaware of cultural cues, or ignorant of popular scams, become targets for con artists and fraudsters. Never hand your passport to anyone, even official-looking people, on the street. Don't turn your back on any personal belongings unless they are chained down. Take multiple copies of your passport (first and last pages and the visa). Extra passport photos may also be required for certain forms once you're in India.

Special Advice for Women

You may simply be being friendly, but easy, open conversation, eye contact, and any kind of physical touch may well be interpreted as a come-on. If you are traveling alone, make friends with another woman or a family near you on the train or bus. Dress modestly, covering legs, arms, and cleavage.

An Indian man may ask to take your photograph, or to have his friend take your picture with him. Such pictures become the background for lies about his "new foreign girlfriend" or his latest sexual conquest. If you don't want to be fantasy material, don't allow your picture to be taken by men.

These things may irritate and anger you, as a woman who is not be accustomed to such treatment. But challenging the system by refusing to act in culturally appropriate ways will not change these men or this negative aspect of India.

Sexual assaults on women are on the rise in India. A recent Reuters Foundation survey has labeled India as "the most dangerous country in the world for women." Be aware of your surroundings and take sensible precautions. The best way to take care of yourself is to adjust to the cultural norms for women and surround yourself with good people—of whom, there are plenty.

CHAPTER EIGHT

BUSINESS BRIEFING

Once viewed as a case study for third-world poverty or seen as an exotic destination for adventurous tourists, India is now the world's one-stop technology shop. Reforms over the past thirty years have liberalized foreign investment, reduced tariffs, opened up the financial sector, and deregulated industry. India has become a global giant, generating wealth and jobs, opening doors to new markets, and providing critical skills for the world economy.

Indian business acumen is nothing new. Sixteen million Indian-born people live as expats. India bemoaned the "brain drain" as many college-educated men and women left to pursue higher education or to join extended family and experience a higher standard of living abroad. Just a few years ago, Indians were the second-largest, and one of the fastest-growing, legal immigrant populations in the US. But not anymore.

Today, reverse immigration is motivated by the very things that spurred emigration in the past. Government initiatives have made it easy for Indians who have relinquished their citizenship or who were born abroad to start businesses and to acquire a lifelong visa.

The reverse immigration of unprecedented numbers of young, competent, and highly educated Indians is also pushing companies in the US and Europe to shift their research and development to India. Many companies outsource technological services or move entire areas of business to India to retain the know-how and expertise being lost in the new migration, as well as to take advantage of the affordability of India's labor force.

These returnees, after years of living, studying, and working in the West, understand Western business practices and Western cultural values. That makes doing business in India more attractive. But corporate and government structures and policies, as well as deeper, usually unspoken values, create tensions that require cross-cultural skill, relational savvy, and additional investment of time and money on the part of the foreign business person.

BUSINESS CULTURE

Hierarchy
Indian business organization charts may look familiar, but there are overlapping structures based on family, caste, and other social dynamics that are not evident.

The CEO and anyone with a recognized title will be given the respect due to their position, regardless of color, caste, or gender. Supervisors are shown respect and obeyed, at least on the surface. Challenging ideas, contradicting opinions, questioning decisions, and saying "no" are not acceptable behavior for underlings. Considerable energy is expended on being agreeable to one's boss. Indians place a high value on pleasing those in authority. In a hierarchy, your position and well-being are contingent on those above you looking good and on those below you being controlled. Employees work hard to meet deadlines, to agree with their superiors, and to avoid making—or revealing—mistakes.

Indians painfully learn as children that they are not allowed to make mistakes. When a mistake happens, it is ignored if possible, hidden when necessary, and fixed at all costs before it can become public. In this shame-based culture, even trivial errors that have no economic fallout have emotional and relational consequences.

Networks

Networks are already established by the time a graduate looks for a job or an entrepreneur starts a business. Family and caste, or community, have supported and directed the individual from birth, and will continue to do so during their career. Relatives often work together. The majority of employees in a business may be from a single caste.

It is also a kind of insurance. Financial assets, special skills, and even family secrets are kept within the family or community. In these homogeneous environments, the broader social ranking and internal family dynamics come into play, with clearly defined roles. Relational entanglements and communal politics, however, can sabotage communication and productivity. Tensions may be felt but not understood by those outside the system.

*COMMON MISTAKES FOREIGNERS
MAKE IN BUSINESS RELATIONSHIPS*

- Treating everyone as an equal.
- Addressing people by their first names.
- Greeting people with a hug or a kiss.
- Offering a contrary opinion.
- Publicly pointing out problems or conflicts in an attempt to solve them.
- Initiating a discussion that requires debate or disclosure of weakness.
- Assuming everyone understands your English.
- Assuming you are getting all the facts.
- Asking for decisions to be made during a meeting.
- Using the same management tools as used in your home country.
- Not including an allowance in project timelines for miles of red tape.
- Offering or receiving money or important documents with the left hand.

Relationships and Time

The relaxed Indian view of time and the relational capital required to get things done should not be mistaken for laziness, carelessness, naivety, or ineptitude. You may feel time is wasted as conversations circle around personal and professional issues, but work is being accomplished. Attempts to drive the discussion in a straight line will bring everything to a halt. Expect to spend time building relationships both with those who appear to have power and with those who do not.

Gatekeepers

In spite of a clear hierarchy, getting things done is not as simple as walking into the top office. A lot of time and effort are required to run around to various offices, fill out forms, get multiple signatures, and secure the goodwill of everyone in the process.

Gatekeepers can be found at every level. It could be the receptionist at the front desk, the clerk with the rubber stamp, the accountant whose signature is required, or the employee who has a relative who can get it done more cheaply. Even for many at the bottom of the food chain, their importance to the system is highlighted by their power to stall or sabotage the process. You will be asked to wait even if it is clear that the person has nothing else to do. You will be told to "come back tomorrow." Tomorrow, when you turn up, you will find the same person doing the same thing he could have completed yesterday.

Resist the urge to engage in a power struggle. As a foreigner you may be allowed to go directly to the boss, but it's best to show respect to everyone you meet on the way.

MEETINGS

Getting Started

E-mails, official memos, and other corporate forms of communication may not be the most effective ways of setting up meetings or making important requests. With younger workers, SMS or WhatsApp may achieve the desired result. But due to the relational nature of doing business, personal invitations or a phone call from the immediate supervisor may be required.

Even at the height of the monsoon season or summer heat, Indians look smart. Starched shirts and striped ties are standard business wear for men. Women are wrapped conservatively in perfectly pleated saris, *shalwar kameez*, or modest dresses. Be sure that you, too, are dressed appropriately when meeting businesspeople.

Punctuality is relative and will depend on the expectations of the corporate leadership. Those in authority may arrive late. Plan on initiating or participating in small talk, including inquiries about family, before getting down to business.

At the Meeting

Indian business meetings, generally speaking, are more like presentations than forums for discussion or collaborative thinking. The senior member speaks his mind, and others seldom speak at all. It is not that they don't have anything to contribute: it is the right of those in authority to speak and the responsibility of others to listen. Indians do not interrupt those in authority. Silence is understood to be acquiescence. Any other response may be viewed as negative.

To contribute as an equal is to engage in a power struggle. Rarely will an employee risk putting his or her idea forward in a group setting. The danger of being shamed is too great. Even in a one-on-one conversation, aggressively pursuing a goal or a direct line of reasoning will create a problem, as one party will believe he has persuaded the other and the other party will be wondering how to get out of the deal without damaging the relationship.

Formal meetings are useful for disseminating information, affirming one's position of power, or communicating instructions. They are not an effective way of generating ideas, understanding employee concerns, evaluating performance, gathering information, or getting real consensus. Rather, time and energy should be spent on regular, informal meetings with individuals.

In the Indian context, respect, listening, acknowledgment of contributions, specific expectations, and clear decisions are important. You may be able to make headway in a meeting by creating clear ground rules for discussion and contribution. But performance reviews, brainstorming sessions, and other Western management tools intended to strengthen performance, spur discussion, correct weaknesses, and build teams may do more harm than good. In India communication is top-down, and creativity and debate are not expected, or desired, in employees.

At the end of a meeting, clearly stated goals and action steps may be well received. But do not expect follow-through without a human connection that will ensure accountability. This is especially true if an employee is unsure of how to proceed, since they are not likely to admit inability to a superior.

Presentations
At the climax of your presentation, when you might expect everyone to be applauding or diving into discussion, you may look around the room to see

blank stares. No one has understood your British or American English and, afraid of embarrassing you and themselves, no one will say so. Because of the many ways in which communication can go awry, repetition and clarification of key points is essential. It is worth asking "Is my English clear?" at regular intervals during your presentation.

Younger urbanized Indians and those educated in the West may be better able to recognize variations in accents and to respond to a more direct, informal management style. But don't assume that superficially familiar behavior on their part, such as addressing you by your first name, or wearing jeans to the office, means that you are properly understood. Adaptations may be based on Western media images. Even those who may be more Westernized in their thinking are still part of a system built around an Indian frame of reference.

Decision Making

Decisions are made by the person with the appropriate title. As long as employees feel that their work is valued and their position is secure, they see no need to share the boss's responsibility. The person required to make the decision may consult peers, specialists, or family members to minimize the risk of a bad decision or of taking the blame for it. Decisions are often based on the criteria of perceived trustworthiness and likeability rather than on competence and track record. Family and strategic relationships are factors when hiring, promoting, or firing.

NEGOTIATIONS

If the person you're dealing with is not the decision maker, then more discussion, documentation, and protocols will be required to get appropriate approvals. Depending on your position, you may be able to go straight to the top. But it's easy to misstep in a complicated hierarchy in which nepotism and caste, or communal loyalties may be at work. Deals can go awry if you unknowingly circumvent someone in power, omit a signature, or choose the wrong go-between.

Expect negotiations and implementation to take much longer than they would at home. Pushing agendas or making demands will only alienate you from those who need to be involved in the process.

CONTRACTS

In India, a written contract may be regarded as fluid— open to adaptation when circumstances or personnel change. It may be viewed as an indicator of an intention established in the context of a prior relationship. Business colleagues, relying on their relationship with you rather than on a piece of paper, may be surprised if you raise an objection or threaten legal action if part of a contract has not been fulfilled. Past conversations may be offered as evidence that different arrangements were made by verbal agreement.

Indian contracts need careful attention on many levels. Though the language will be English, clarification may be needed because of differing word usage. Smaller companies may not use lawyers to draft or negotiate contracts, so these can read very differently from the highly formal legal documents normal in the West. Different perceptions of what constitutes a key point can lead to confusing conversations, calling for patience and flexible thinking. A foreign company will need to establish clearly the specific laws that govern a contract and its arbitration. For matters relating to intellectual property, "work for hire," liability, and taxes you will need the help of a qualified lawyer.

CORRUPTION

Corruption continues to plague India. Despite the economic reforms, India's huge bureaucracies create barriers that many choose to overcome by means of bribery. Red tape can make registering a company, getting a tax ID number, or dealing with banks a slow process. Obstinate officials may extort *baksheesh* to move your request forward or to turn on standard services, such as electricity. Kickbacks, are widespread in government, education, and business.

India pays a high price for these practices: an estimated US $1 trillion a year. But the loss is not merely monetary. Business, people development, and justice are hindered by corrupt practices. Sadly, a bribe is often more expedient and less confusing than the hassle that can be created by clerks, bureaucrats, police officers, government officials, and school administrators. While such "tips," bribes, and gifts are not the only way to get things done, you and your company will have to decide how to handle this common facet of "business as usual" in India.

COLLEAGUES

Day-to-Day Communication
Ask colleagues how best to stay in touch. E-mail, which may be the preferred means of business communication back home, may only be checked intermittently by your Indian associates, who may be more used to phone conversations, SMS, and WhatsApp.

Communication should be direct and personal. Official paper reports or e-mail communications will probably convey what you want to hear rather than what's actually being done. Face-to-face is best. When that's not possible, virtual conversations or phone contact can help build or maintain the relational capital needed to get the job done. But, like anywhere, be sure to have e-mail documentation of conversations, requests, and decisions made. Follow up on important issues or implementation details in person.

Working Together
"Able to work independently" is not something you're likely to see on a job description in India. Competence matters, but dependability and loyalty matter more. Employees may be expected to help one another meet deadlines or to provide skills, or connections that are lacking. Decisions are rarely made alone. Consulting and consensus protect an employee from being blamed when a decision leads to failure. Colleagues want to know that their workmates can be counted on to help them succeed, to make them look good to superiors, and to cover for them when mistakes are made.

While many have the drive to excel and everyone wants to be acknowledged for work done well, to be singled out for attention, even when it's positive, creates difficulties. For example, giving a raise based on performance, rather than seniority, may create dissatisfaction in the ranks. High performers may have to deal with their colleagues' jealousy, which can damage relationships and prospects.

These and other stressful aspects of Indian business culture can stifle initiative and independent thought. On the other hand, they have compelled frustrated and enterprising individuals to strike out on their own, creating new businesses and opportunities for many.

MANAGING CONFLICT

Two words are the key here: conflict avoidance. Transparency is difficult to find. Indians do not criticize others to their face. Ideas are not challenged. Differences of opinion are not voiced. You will hear what they think you want to hear. Even if you ask for honest input you probably won't get it, if it is deemed to be negative. Most Indians appreciate practical Western problem solving, organizational skills, and a "can-do" attitude; but those same qualities can create tension. If you step into a workplace to identify problems or suggest ways to enhance efficiency, you may be perceived as arrogant. If colleagues are reluctant to take action, do not mistake this for incompetence or apathy. Rifts can widen because no one will risk the relationship to address tensions.

It may be possible to have a conversation about conflict in the workplace if this is done privately. Be humble about your role and honest about your desire for resolution. Assure your colleagues that you will not use what they say against them. If they trust you they may open up. If not, change your strategy. Listen to what they say about others for clues about their values, their pressure points, their expectations, and, perhaps, how these relate to you. Then it's up to you to adjust your expectations and behavior.

WOMEN IN BUSINESS

There are strong, capable women at all levels of business and government in India. Fourteen percent of the country's entrepreneurs are women. Even so, the pressures of family obligations, fears of sexual harassment, and assumptions about limitations prevent many from being employed in some professions, or offered advancement, or even entering the marketplace.

Generally women in business are treated with respect, but there are few Indian women in upper management positions. Western women tend to be treated more as a male peer might be. Depending on the company, and those in authority, women doing business in India may well enlist male help to communicate, negotiate, and ensure implementation of decisions. India's relational and hierarchical style of doing business requires the kind of one-on-one conversation and socializing that's still not possible between the sexes in India.

CHAPTER NINE

COMMUNICATING

LANGUAGE

Language Families and Factions

Experts differ on the number of languages spoken in India. Officially, the government recognizes twenty-two, but 1,950 have been identified. Most Indian languages derive from two linguistic families: Indo–Aryan and Dravidian. Hindi in its various forms comes from Indo–Aryan-based Sanskrit, and is the primary language of 44 percent of India's people. The Dravidian-based languages of South India—Tamil, Telugu, Malayalam, and Kannada—are spoken by 19 percent. Languages spoken in the northeast and on India's islands, are unrelated Sino–Tibetan and Austro–Asiatic languages.

Most educated Indians speak two, if not three, four, or five languages. While English is commonly used in business, and is the preferred medium of education, especially for the middle and upper classes, Indians have strong feelings related to their mother tongue. In recent years, regions and states have asserted their linguistic rights and cultural identities by reassigning original names to more than 100 major cities. Calcutta is now Kolkata (Bengali); Bombay is Mumbai (Marathi); Bangalore is Bangaluru (Kannada); Madras is Chennai (Tamil); and Cochin is Kochi (Malayalam). Growing demands for self-rule by various ethno-linguistic groups could well lead to the formation of many new states by 2050.

Whose English?

The history of politics and education combined with current global business opportunities have motivated Indians to continue to learn to read, write, and speak English—but this may be a different English from yours.

Indian children are still taught the King's English. Educated Indians have excellent English and can be very articulate. But Indian English, which evolved during the British Raj, has some idiosyncrasies.

English and its Indian variants are spoken or written not just on the job or in the club, but on TV, in movies, and in contemporary literature. There are purists who argue for a return to precolonial languages, but the English tsunami hit India long ago, and waves of Indian English, or "Hinglish," and IT-trained Americanisms and accents continue to pour into India.

Language Learning

Most people in urban India speak at least basic English. But, because of the inextricable link between language and identity, any effort you make to learn a few basic phrases will be appreciated by those you meet. So ask questions, take a few linguistic risks, laugh at and learn

---

IT'S INDIAN ENGLISH, ISN'T IT?

Isn't it?	Isn't that the case? (at the end of a sentence)
Tell me	I'm listening, or Can I help you?
I'll try	I can't (but I don't want to hurt your feelings).
Yes	No, in answer to questions stated in the negative: "Aren't you going?" or "Didn't you do it?" (Yes, I am not going, or I didn't do it)."
What to do?	Nothing can be done about it.
Off it	Turn it off.
Good name	Full name
Out of station	Out of town
Healthy	Fat
Hotel	Restaurant
Prepone	Move an appointment earlier
Shifting	Moving
Simply	Just, or just like that

from your mistakes. Enjoy the beauty of India's languages and the people who speak them.

GREETINGS

In this traditional society, how you greet others matters. Respect, relationship, religion, and social status are communicated in greetings. In many arenas today handshakes, especially between men, are acceptable. With a woman, it's best to use the traditional "*Namaste*" or "Hello" with the hand posture and a smile. Only shake her hand if she extends it first. Europeans and Americans should not greet members of the opposite sex with a kiss or a hug.

BODY LANGUAGE

Trying to read body language and watch social cues in India can exasperate an outsider. Much of what is communicated is nonverbal. It's easy to misunderstand or miss something altogether. If you think you've missed something important, ask an Indian to explain; but they've probably read the situation without having to think about it, so they may not know what you're talking about.

Don't be confused by the side-to-side head bob. You may think someone is shaking their head to mean "no," but it means "yes," or "I hear you," and sometimes "thank you."

Finger pointing is rude. Gesturing in a direction is done either with the chin or by using the whole hand. To sign to someone to come to you, hold your hand palm down and wave your fingers. Beckoning with palm up is inappropriate, as are winking, whistling, and singing, which can be interpreted as sexual come-ons.

COMMON GREETINGS AND GESTURES

North Indian Hindus

"*Namaste*." Place palms together, with hands held in front of your chest. (You don't need to bow—it's not done in India.) The hand gesture alone is a respectful greeting, especially when you enter a roomful of people.

Pranam is a more formal gesture that you'll observe in north India. With fingertips, one touches the feet of a parent, elder family member, or other respected person. It is often followed by putting one's hand on one's heart or head, acknowledging that this person has the power to bless.

South Indians

"Hello" is "*Namaskara*" (Kannada), "*Namasakaram*" (Malayalam, Telugu), or "*Vanakham*" (Tamil), accompanied by the traditional "*namaste*" hand gesture, handshake, or briefly touching hand to chest.

Muslims

"*Assalaam alaikum*" ("peace be upon you")
Reply: "*Alaikum salaam*" ("upon you be peace")

Signs of Respect

Signs of respect are important. Women may be expected to cover their heads when entering religious places or if they are present when prayers are being said in someone's home. Not making direct eye contact is a sign, too, to elders that you are giving them due respect. Shoes are unclean. Never put them on a table or other furniture. Removing shoes to enter a home or a holy place is a given. You may choose to keep your socks on, if you're wearing any, but bare feet are the norm. Sometimes a shoe or a *chappal* (sandal) is used by a woman to threaten a man who is doing something shameful.

HUMOR

One needs only to look at Indian cinema to begin to grasp the place of humor in India and to see what Indians find funny. From broad physical comedy to subtle verbal exchanges or offhand remarks, even serious Indian movies are laced with laughs. Slapstick and parody are typically what foreigners understand as "Indian humor," since other forms of humor and its nuances cannot be understood without knowing the language and learning the culture.

It may appear that nothing is sacred in Indian comedy. Social relationships, subcultures, caste and class, social ills, holy men, physical traits—all are mocked and satirized by comedians in film, on TV, in comedy clubs, and by groups of young people just having fun. With a growing global Indian Diaspora, Indian comedy expresses their cross-cultural realities and internal struggles.

Not all humor translates across cultures. There are forms to avoid if you don't want to be misunderstood. Sarcasm will certainly offend. Self-deprecating humor will be viewed as a statement of fact about yourself that may return to haunt you.

Trying to ease tension by making light of a person or problem will be interpreted as a put-down. Although many cultures have jokes about specific subcultures, *Sardar* (Sikh) jokes, the Indian equivalent of "blonde" jokes in the US, are best avoided. Caricature is a common form of comedy in film and even between friends, but Indians do not poke fun at, or joke around with, parental figures, bosses, or anyone deemed above them in the social order.

MEDIA AND TECHNOLOGY

Not only interpersonal and business relationships, but lifestyle and culture are changing radically as India's consumers and companies connect globally to goods, education, business, and opportunities in, and through, technology. Indians continue to be the largest providers of IT outsourcing in the world and the fastest-growing market for technology-related goods and services.

The Press

Not everything has been taken over by technological advances. While the West turns from the printed page to TV and the Internet, most Indians still get their news from newspapers. India's 105,450 newspapers have a whopping readership of 407 million. The Indian press is independent and privately owned. Editors and TV chiefs appear to exercise self-censorship and intentionally minimize crises and underestimate the numbers injured and dead in a conflict in efforts to prevent the escalation of further violence.

Air Waves

Fifty percent of the population owns a TV. In this interconnected and highly social society, neighbors and relatives often watch special programs together.

In the past Indian television was dominated by Doordarshan, India's government-owned TV station, which used the cultural love of the arts and visual media, and the tendency of the uneducated in India to perceive what they saw on the small screen as reality, to promote certain political views. But in 1990 the Prasar Bharati Act required an independent Broadcasting Corporation to be established to regulate both TV and radio broadcasting.

A year later, satellite TV exploded on to the Indian TV scene. Now nearly nine hundred TV stations broadcast across India. Sports, soaps, religious sagas, contests, dramas, comedies, and news programs are available in every major language. Through both TV and the Internet, Indians are being exposed to ways of living and thinking that challenge traditional patterns.

Internet

India is wired. The proliferation of outsourcing companies—IT businesses, computer training centers, and Internet cafés—indicates the e-change that's happening.

Even though 66 percent of India's population does not have access to the Internet, India ranks second in the world in Internet use, with 450 million users. Networks exist in and around major cities, but connections can be sketchy or just plain slow.

Blackouts are not uncommon, so make sure you keep battery packs for cell phones and laptops topped up.

If you carry a laptop, cell phone, or e-reader, remember to take an adaptor that fits Indian 230 volt, 50 Hz outlets. USB-based Wi-Fi devices are available from several carriers inside India at a modest price. But if you need repairs, service centers outside major cities will be hard to find.

Telephone

India ranks second in the world in cell phone sales and production (behind China), and in the number of smartphone users (after the US). Of India's 650 million cell phone users, 300 million own smartphones. Though English-based smartphones pose a language barrier for a majority, India has the fastest growing smartphone market on the planet.

Many American wireless phone services are accessible around India and prepaid phones and SIM cards are readily available.

Mail

India Post boasts the world's largest postal system. Its 155,000 offices, most of which are located outside the cities, also serve as banks for rural India. Declining business in the past decade has resulted in office closures and a reduction in the number of employees.

Speed post, money orders, bill payment, e-Post, and international fund transfers (including e-payment) can all be done at the post office.

CONCLUSION

All descriptions of "India" or "Indians" can only be offered as a simplification to aid understanding, rather than as a complete representation. That's both the beauty and the challenge of visiting India—there is little that can be labeled generically as "Indian culture." And there is little that compares with our own life "back home," at least beyond the superficial trappings acquired during the British Raj or under the influence of MTV.

India has conquered conquerors, illuminated artists, inspired sages, fueled invention, and is today changing the face and the future of our world. Indians have a joke about the extent of their influence, saying that when the first spaceship landed on the moon, the astronauts heard "*Chai! Chai!*" and stepped out to find an Indian selling tea from a cart. That is a good picture of the reality of India: still doing things the old way, yet paradoxically far ahead of everyone else.

Daily life for most still follows the patterns set by previous generations, focused on caring for family and, if fate allows, preparing one's children for a better future. Fatalism and the synthesis of the Hindu concepts of *karma* (we get what we deserve) and *maya* (what we see is not real) affects all of India's cultures, giving Indians a capacity to live with social inequity and personal hardship without having to manage it, excuse it, or pretend it isn't there.

Life is made both difficult and predictable by the still dominant system of caste. Everyone knows their place, and options are determined by community, gender, and the social pecking order. But in ways that were unthinkable even a decade ago, those barriers are being broken down. Doors to education and a better future are slowly being opened by law, economic reform, globalization, technological advancement, media, and a seismic cultural shift that is already shaking India's ancient footing.

The intensity and diversity of India can create both shock and awe for visitors that are not likely to subside. India is an experience best appreciated by those who are open to learn, able to cope with ambiguity, and willing to redefine generosity and friendship. Falling in love with India is much like developing a taste for spicy food. You look at the chilies and don't know how you'll cope. But the aroma is enticing, so you dive in. If you don't give up, one day you'll discover that you've developed a craving for it.

> **India of the ages is not dead, nor has she spoken her last creative word; she lives and has still something to do for herself and the human peoples.**
> *Sri Aurobindo*

FURTHER READING

Bhagat, Chetan. *What Young India Wants.* New Delhi: Rupa Publications India Pvt. Ltd, 2015.

———. *Two States: The Story of My Marriage.* Kolkata: Rupa Publications Pvt Ltd, 2009.

Boo, Katherine. *Behind the Beautiful Forevers.* London: Portobello Books Ltd, 2014.

Gandhi, Mohandas. *An Autobiography: My Experiments with Truth.* London: Penguin Classics, 2001.

Guha, Ramachandra. I*ndia after Gandhi: The History of the World's Largest Democracy.* London/New York: Harper Perennial, 2008.

Kakar, Sudhir and Katharina. *The Indians, The Portrait of a People.* London: SAB, 2011.

Kalsi, Sewa Singh. *Sikhism.* London: Simple Guides, 2007.

Kamdar, Mira. *Planet India: How the Fastest-Growing Democracy is Transforming America and the World.* New York: Scribner, 2008.

Lewis, Richard D. *When Cultures Collide: Managing Successfully Across Cultures.* London: Nicholas Brealey Publishing, 1999.

O'Reilly, James P., and Larry Habegger (eds.). *India.* San Francisco, California: Travelers' Tales, 1995.

Radjou, Navi, and Jaideep Prabhu, Simone Ahuja. *Jugaad Innovation, Think Frugal, Be Flexible, Generate Breakthrough Growth.* San Francisco: Jossey-Bass, 2012.

Roy, Arundhati. *The God of Small Things.* London: Harper Perennial, 1997.

Sen, Amertya. *The Argumentative Indian: Writings on Indian History, Culture and Identity.* London: Picador, 2006.

Singh, Khushwant. *Train to Pakistan.* New Delhi: Penguin Books India, 1994.

Tagore, Rabindranath. *Gora.* Kolkata: Rupa Publications Pvt Ltd, 2002.

Abram, David, et al. *The Rough Guide to India.* London: Rough Guides, 2001.

PICTURE CREDITS

Cover Image: *Decorated Indian elephant in front of Buland Darwaza Fatehpur Sikri Agra at sunset.* © Shutterstock/Roop_Dey.

Canva: pages 38 by green aperture; 39 by Noppasin; 48 by rajatk; 118 by rawpixel.com; 136 by monstArrr_; 170 by Kishrej.

Pixabay: pages 12 by Free-Photos; 17 by Prabhjit S. Katsi; 70 by shilpasing369; 77 by Free-Photos; 102 by pictureperfect7; 107 by elgroot; 123 by saumendra.

Images on these pages are reproduced under:

Creative Commons Attribution 2.0 Generic license: 23 ©Dharma from Sadao, Thailand; 75 © CC-BY; 86 © Nico Crisafulli.

Creative Commons Attribution-Share Alike 2.0 Generic license: 40 © MM; 54 © MM; 73 © dhondusaxena; 126 © Adam Jones from Kelowna, BC, Canada; 130 © Diganta Talukdar; 144 © Navin Thakur; 150 © Shizhao.

Creative Commons Attribution-Share Alike 3.0 Unported license: 7 © Addicted04; 46 © Purshi; 82 © Ibrahim Husain Meraj; 128 © Techkriti; 184 © Shajankumar.

Creative Commons Attribution-Share Alike 4.0 International license: 24 © Chrisi 1964; 27 ©Bikashrd; 90 © Hemant banswal; 111 © Foisaluddin5241; 114 © Parag Gore.

Creative Commons Attribution-Share Alike 4.0 International, 3.0 Unported, 2.5 Generic, 2.0 Generic and 1.0 Generic license: 55 © Paulrudd; 133 © Dhirad.

INDEX

Acknowledgments

Many thanks to: Mom for faith; Jo for confidence; Geoffrey for kindness; friends and colleagues for insight; Josh for companionship and comic relief; my Indian family for allowing me to belong; and Roy (you know what for). And to my fan club (you know who you are) who promised to buy and use my book. Here it is!